I0151936

How to Ace Your Business Finance Class:

Essential Knowledge and Techniques to Master the Material and Ace your Exams

How to Ace Your Business Finance Class:

Essential Knowledge and Techniques to Master the Material and Ace your Exams

Timothy Falcon Crack
PhD (MIT), MCom, PGDipCom,
BSc (HONS 1st Class), IMC

©2018 TIMOTHY FALCON CRACK

All rights reserved worldwide. No part of this book may be reproduced, stored in a retrieval system, or transmitted in any form or by any means, electronic, mechanical, photocopying, recording, or otherwise, without the prior written permission of the author.

Warning: The author accepts no liability in any event including (without limitation) negligence for any damages or loss of any kind, including (without limitation) direct, indirect, incidental, special or consequential damages, expenses or losses arising out of, or in connection with, your use or inability to use the information in this book.

Published by: Timothy Falcon Crack, P.O. Box 6385, Dunedin North, Dunedin 9059, New Zealand.

Cover images: United States coin images from the United States Mint (used with permission).

Third edition, March 2018 (Revised)
ISBN: 978-0-9941386-5-1

Typeset by the author.
FoundationsForScientificInvesting.com/books.htm
timcrack@alum.mit.edu

Contents

Preface

This book is aimed at students in their first finance class at the undergraduate, MBA, or executive education (exec-ed) level. The class is usually called "Business Finance" or "Financial Management."

My goals are to help you master the material and to lift your grades. I approach these goals from two different angles. First, I use 25 years of experience teaching this material to explain carefully the stumbling blocks that have consistently tripped up students year after year. Addressing these common sources of confusion gives every student every opportunity to master the material. Second, I present safe strategies I have developed to help you solve numerical problems. Although these strategies take only an extra minute to implement, they frame each numerical problem so as to increase the likelihood that you detect and fix any errors, while reducing the likelihood that you make any errors in the first place. These techniques also increase the likelihood that you earn partial credit—if your instructor offers it.

Note that because I focus on stumbling blocks, I necessarily skip over some simpler material that does not usually cause problems. As such, I do not cover every topic in the class—that is what your actual textbook, lectures, and lecture notes are for. Similarly, I give only enough worked examples to explain concepts and techniques. You should look to your textbook for additional worked examples.

I recognize that different students have different needs. For example, you might have no real interest in finance, but you need to pass the class to get your degree. Alternatively, you might be a gung-ho finance major who wants to ace the class, or an MBA or exec-ed student who does not care about grades, and just wants to master the material. I have been meeting different needs in the classroom for 25 years, and my presentation here is pitched simultaneously to these different clienteles.

Am I the right person to be your tutor? I think my experience makes me a good choice:

- I taught this class to more than 3,000 freshmen

over a recent 10-year period. I also taught the same material to thousands of students as parts of other classes over a previous 15-year period.

- In my 25 years of teaching this material, I have noticed that students consistently stumble over exactly the same parts of the class every year. As part of my job, I have spent 25 years developing good ways of countering these common mistakes. I am a committed teacher who has won six university teaching awards and been nominated for at least five others (for teaching this class and others).

- I did PhD coursework in Finance at MIT and Harvard, and I graduated with a PhD in Financial Economics from MIT. I have degrees in Mathematics (with a lot of Statistics), Finance, and Financial Economics and a diploma in Accounting/Finance. I also hold the Investment Management Certificate (IMC) from the U.K. Society of Investment Professionals.

- I have published in the top academic journal in Finance (*The Journal of Finance*), the top practitioner-oriented journals in Finance (*The Financial Analysts Journal* and *The Journal of*

Futures Markets), and the top pedagogical journal in Finance (*The Journal of Financial Education*). I have also published in what was the top interdisciplinary business journal (*The Journal of Business*). I have written six other sole-authored finance books which have sold very well with good reviews (see advertisements at the end of this book).

- I taught at the university level from 1985 to 2000, and again from 2004 onwards, rising from a teaching assistant to a chaired full professor. My experience includes four years as a front line teaching assistant for MBA students studying finance at MIT, and about five years teaching undergraduate, MBA, and PhD classes in finance at Indiana University's Kelley School of Business (then ranked in the top five in the U.S. for undergraduate finance, top 20 in the U.S. for general MBA programs, and top 10 in the U.S. for PhD programs in finance).

- I have worked as an independent consultant to the New York Stock Exchange (NYSE) and to a foreign government body investigating wrongdoing in the financial markets. I have also run a successful internet-based small business since

1995, and I have traded in the equity, equity options, index options, and index/commodity/FX ETF markets for 20 years. My most recent practitioner job was as the head of quantitative active equity research for the U.K. and Continental Europe in the London office of what was the world's largest institutional asset manager.

My unique background of learning, teaching, consulting, trading, and practice is reflected on every page. There can be no guarantee that you will pass with my help, because the material is difficult by nature for many students, however, by pointing out where thousands of students before you have stumbled, and by using my award-winning teaching experience to address these stumbling blocks, I am hopeful that I can help you to master the material and avoid common mistakes.

Although this book is aimed primarily at students, the fact that I focus on essential knowledge and techniques also makes this book useful to instructors. For example, an instructor who is new to the class can use this book to quickly improve his or her understanding and teaching of the trickiest parts.

I thank the thousands of undergraduate students who were guinea pigs for the classroom testing of the material in this book over a period of 25 years. Some of the content on capital budgeting benefited from my exposure to material presented by Kevin Rock when I was his teaching assistant in a case-based corporate finance class at MIT. I also benefited from being allowed to sit in on investment banking candidate interviews, either in person or via video conference, at a bulge bracket investment bank for the 10 years 2005–2014. I also thank Scott Chaput, Robin Grieves, Ming Yang Li, Mitchell McCutcheon, Olena Onishchenko, Helen Roberts, Avinash Shastri, and Christine Smith-Han for discussions, assistance, or feedback. Any errors are my own.

If, after reading this book and making an honest effort with the material, you find that your understanding and your grades have improved, then please go to **Amazon.com** and leave a positive review for this book so that other people may similarly benefit from it. Just type the ISBN number from the back cover into Amazon's Web site and then click on the box labeled "Write a customer review." Thank you.

TFC/2018

Tables

Figures

Introduction

With little effort you can use this book to improve your grades a little. "Little effort" is not, however, going to be enough if you are a nervous student needing to push your grade up to a safe pass, or if you are an ace student seeking an "A+." So, I invite you to follow the "Lincoln Approach" (see p. 4), and to then jump in and embrace the material.

In my review of the class material, I have broken the topics up into bite-sized chapters. One very common mistake among students is, however, to view the topics in these chapters as sitting in separate silos. Students skip a class or a chapter, not realizing how interdependent the topics are.

Let me give some examples. The CAPM has a chapter to itself, but the CAPM can be used to help estimate the cost of capital, and the CAPM also ties in with the discussion of risk and return, and with the discussion of diversification. Discussion of both the cost of equity and capital structure feeds into discount rates for capital budgeting decision rules, and the cost of equity feeds into dividend discount models for stock valuation. The chapter on free cash flow (FCF) estimation feeds directly into capital budgeting decision rules in the numerator of a net present value (NPV) calculation, say, with discount rates in the denominator. To understand FCF you need some degree of comfort with the structure of the financial statements, discussed briefly in another chapter; the financial statements, in turn, tie in with the discussion of capital structure. Also, both stock valuation and capital budgeting decision rules require the use of the material in the time value of money chapters (TVM I and TVM II); so too does bond valuation. The dividend policy discussion ties in with equity valuation and also with risk and return, and also with the introductory chapter that discusses shareholder wealth maximization, which in turn ties in with the capital budgeting chapters. I could go on, but suffice it to say that almost every topic in the class is linked in some way to almost every other topic in the class.

Students who fail to see the linkages between the

topics, and who choose to skip one or two topics, ultimately have difficulty seeing the big picture and passing the class. Given these inter-relationships, my advice is that you skip as little as possible, and preferably nothing.

Because the topics/chapters are so interdependent, I have little choice but to mention some later chapter topics in earlier chapters. When I do so, I tread lightly and point to the later chapter where more depth will appear.

I usually introduce each chapter with a little background material. Sometimes this is something of a history lesson to frame the topic. Other times it is just a motivation for a topic, or an explanation of some key intuition.

I sometimes refer to material beyond the usual content of the class. It might be a topic at a higher level, or perhaps in accounting or economics, or a topic that does not apply to the U.S., etc. I am doing this mostly for those students who want to be "A+" students, or who plan to major in finance, or who are MBA or exec-ed students. If you are a struggling undergraduate student just trying to achieve a passing grade, you can ignore these extra comments, if you wish; they are the only things you should skip, and they are clearly labeled.

The Lincoln Approach

Many non-finance majors are fearful of the mathematics in this class. Let me turn to President Abraham Lincoln's words. When the Civil War was almost over, and the South was nearly defeated, Abraham Lincoln was advised to *destroy* the South. He refused to do so and replied with something like "Do we not destroy our enemies by making them our friends?" That is, rather than destroy the Southerners, he thought they should be embraced. After all, once they have been embraced as friends, they are destroyed as enemies.

Abraham Lincoln's words apply surprisingly widely. For example, I often need to master a new finance topic, a new mathematical technique, a new piece of software, etc. At first I may feel that I am facing an enemy, but I jump into the new challenge and I embrace it. I wallow around in my ignorance for a little while. Soon I begin to see some patterns. Shortly after that, some concepts begin to gel, and then, after some honest work, I master the material, destroying my "enemy."

I invite you to follow the Lincoln Approach: Set aside your fears or prejudices, jump in and embrace the material, and make your enemy your friend!

Chapter 1

Foundations

Forms of Business

It is difficult to understand forms of business without already having discussed equities (also called "stocks" or "shares"), bonds (a type of fixed-income security or "debt" security), financial statements, capital budgeting, and capital structure. I think the best way to introduce forms of business is via a personal story.

In 1995, I launched an internet-based small business while I was still a student; it was a self-publishing business for the first book I had written. My classmates were talking about the wonderful future of the Internet for business practice, but they told me that I was the only person they knew who was actually exploiting it! Over the subsequent years, my book publishing business has remained small enough that I can run it by myself while also working a regular job. So, my publishing business is, and always has been, a "sole proprietorship." I am the sole (i.e., only) proprietor.

I could, however, easily have grown my business. I could have offered to publish books written by other people in addition to my own book. I could have charged authors a setup fee and taken a cut of their sales revenues. If I had done that, I might have chosen to launch a partnership with my editor to make sure the end product was of consistently high quality, sharing the profits with her. If we had continued to grow, at some stage I might have wanted to raise extra capital (discussed shortly) to take over the printing and distribution currently being outsourced. If loans from friends and family were insufficient, I could have taken out a bank loan. If that was not enough, I might have formed a company, and then sold shares to friends, keeping some shares for myself, paid myself a salary and paid dividends on the shares of my investor friends (an *unlisted* firm is said to be "privately held"). If the company had continued to grow, I might have brought in another manager to help me run it, borrowed more money from non-bank investors, perhaps by issuing bonds, possibly even listing the stock on one of the lesser-regulated stock exchanges for startup companies. Ultimately, I might have sold my listed shares of stock for a lump sum to some other investor, and exited the business, leaving others to run it and others to enjoy the future profits. Anyone could then buy stock (i.e., a slice of ownership) in the company by purchasing shares on the stock exchange, with day-to-day operations run by the manager(s) in place. This story is, roughly speaking, how many well known companies have come into existence.

I chose, however, not to expand my business. So, I am the sole proprietor, and all after-tax profits are mine. My business income therefore feeds into the taxable income on my personal tax forms each year. That is great when a business is making profits. If I make a big loss, however, and end up owing money to friends, the bank, or other creditors, then, if I cannot pay it back, my creditors can petition to have me declared bankrupt, and they can take my house, my car, etc. to settle the bill. That lack of protection of personal assets (i.e., "unlimited liability") can be a real worry to a sole proprietor.

Creating a "limited liability" company, however, protects my personal assets in the event that the business fails. A company is a separate "legal person" in its own right, and if it falls on hard times, and loses money and ends up with creditors, nobody can reach into *my* wallet to recover those funds.

Another downside to a sole proprietorship is that you cannot get an ownership stake without having to also run the business. At the same time, you cannot easily sell your ownership stake. A corporate form coupled with a stock exchange listing addresses both these issues: Stock in listed companies can easily be purchased without the investor also having the burden of acting as a manager (e.g., I own some shares in Apple, but I have no interest in personally running the company); and, as mentioned above, owners of listed stocks can easily sell their ownership stake. A stock exchange listing also gives a ready market for a follow-up issue (called a "seasoned issue") of stock to raise additional capital/funds for further business expansion.

Unlike my sole proprietorship, however, as a stockholder in a company, I worry about whether the managers are running the company for my benefit as a stockholder, or whether they are driving around in limousines, flying first class, spending excessively on lavish expense accounts, and generally just extracting perquisites (i.e., "perks") at my expense. This is an example of a "principal-versus-agent" relationship.

As a stockholder, I am the "principal," and each manager is supposed to act as my "agent" in executing my wishes. To keep the agents' goals aligned with the principals' goals, there is usually some sort of monitoring of the managers (e.g., auditors looking at accounting statements, or large activist shareholders pressuring managers). In addition, some managers may be partly paid in stock to help align their goals with those of the stockholders.

There is a natural tension between stockholders and bondholders. For example, bondholders worry about managers taking actions that favor the stockholders while emptying assets out of the company at the bondholders' expense. In this case, bondholders are the principals and managers are the agents. For example, bondholders do not want the managers to declare an extraordinarily large dividend to stockholders if it materially reduces the ability of the company to pay back its debt obligations.

Similarly, bondholders do not want managers of a company that is near to bankruptcy/insolvency to plow all its funds into an extraordinarily risky project. Doing so may yield a lottery-like pay-off to the shareholders. That is, the shareholders may profit greatly if the risky project is successful, but be no worse off if the project fails (which is the most likely outcome for a lottery ticket holder!). The bondholders, on the other hand, are likely only slightly better off with a successful risky project, and are much worse off with a failure. So, the bondholders usually include provisions (called "debt covenants") in their contracts to stop managers acting against bondholder interests.

Stocks and bonds have different risk-return profiles. This is because stockholders are owners of all residual assets and cash flows, but only *after* any payments owed to bondholders and other creditors. This means that when a company performs very well, the stockholders' share certificates might double or triple in value, but the bondholders' investment returns are limited only to what they were promised (i.e., interest payments plus a return of the principal). Conversely, when a company performs very poorly, stockholders' share certificates might be worth only pennies on the dollar, whereas bondholders, who rank ahead of stockholders, might get back most, but not all, of their investment. Thus, bonds are attractive investments because they are often less risky than stocks, whereas stocks are attractive investments because they carry more upside potential than bonds.[1]

How do managers make decisions on behalf of the suppliers of capital (i.e., stockholders and bondholders)? One way is to use capital budgeting to provide a framework for evaluating proposed investments (e.g., new plant and equipment, expansion of the business, etc.). Capital budgeting is internal corporate investment decision making on a budget.

Once shares of stock are traded on a stock exchange, we have to ask ourselves whether the prices are fair. That is, do the stock market prices reflect the fair value of the ownership interest that they represent? This comes down to the valuation mechanism (the discounting of future forecast cash flows by market participants *en masse*) and the inputs

---

[1]Finance majors should note that although the statements in this paragraph are generally correct, they are not exhaustive. For example, if a company falls into severe distress, even the bondholders might get back only pennies on the dollar. Similarly, if a company recovers from severe distress, its bonds might easily double or triple in value. That is because bonds in a severely distressed company can be quite stocklike. Also, comparisons across companies can yield different sorts of results. For example, the stock in a very healthy company might be expected to be a safer investment than the bonds in a very unhealthy company.

to that mechanism (Do we have the correct cash flows? Do we know the discount rate?). This leads us to a discussion of stock valuation techniques and also "market efficiency" (i.e., whether market prices reflect relevant information).

Given the above-mentioned riskiness of individual stocks, a natural next step would be to discuss the benefits of diversified portfolios of stocks. For example, combining 500 different stocks in a portfolio might mean that poor performance at one company is offset by good performance at another, thus washing out the idiosyncratic risks associated with individual stocks, while leaving behind the systematic risk of the broad economy.

So, starting with the launch of a small sole proprietorship, we have talked about competing forms of business, formation of a corporation, listing on a stock exchange, principal-versus-agent considerations, capital budgeting, valuation, market efficiency, and diversification. That is a good introduction to the class.

Let me conclude this section by pointing out something that I have never heard anyone else say. When I was a student in first-year accounting and finance classes 30 years ago, I have to say that I found the material kind of dull and seemingly unimportant. I have, however, been running a successful small business for just over 20 years now, and I can tell you that fully one half of what I do in my small business involves basic accounting and finance from those first-year classes—especially as they apply to the calculation of revenues, expenses, and subsequent taxes (both domestic and foreign). I could pay someone else to do my taxes for me, but that would cost at least $5,000 per annum. That is expensive for a small business. Besides which, I would still have to collect together the paper trail of source documents and explain the details to the accountant. So, I might as well just do it all myself anyway. Doing my own books also means that I monitor the health of my small business in intimate detail.

I believe that at least half of all small businesses fail in the first five years and at least two-thirds fail within 10 years. I think one of the reasons for these failures is that many entrepreneurs have a great idea for a product or service, but they are terrible at the basic accounting/finance side of things. The end result is that they run their businesses into the ground because of cash flow and/or tax reasons.

So, if you find the material in this class kind of dull, or you think it unimportant, keep in mind that like me, you may surprise yourself and find that you are running a small business in the future. In that case, you may find that you need to use some of the content of this class to keep your head above water.

What is Capital?

A business needs capital to operate. Capital comes in several forms. There is financial capital in the form of money raised for investment (e.g., personal loans in a sole proprietorship, bank loans, funds raised from the issue of stocks and bonds, etc.). There is real capital in the form of physical assets that produce (e.g., plant and equipment, trucks, computers, etc.). There is also human capital (e.g., research expertise in a small start-up tech firm) and intangible capital (e.g., patents, trademarks, brands, and goodwill).

What is Finance?

Finance, in a nutshell, is decision making with money and capital.

The field of finance is often broken up into corporate finance (also called "financial management") and investments (also called "capital markets").

Corporate finance is conducted inside a company, looking out at the world (e.g., What shall we invest our capital in? Shall we pay dividends? How much debt should we issue relative to equity?). Investments is conducted outside the company looking in (e.g., Which companies should we invest in? Should we buy their stock or their bonds? What proportions of each should we hold? What alternative investments should we invest in?).

The majority of this class is concerned with corporate finance. So, let us discuss the overarching objective of a corporation.

Business Objectives

If I am a shareholder, what should be the objective of the manager in running the company on my behalf? You have likely already been told that the answer is *shareholder wealth maximization* (SWM).

There are, however, many possible corporate goals. For example, managers should be treating the employees well, respecting the environment, being a responsible corporate citizen, thinking about both short-term and long-term profitability, etc. Indeed, in some countries, the explicit objective of the managers of the company is satisfaction of *multiple stakeholder welfare* considerations along these lines. Let me call this latter concept "stakeholder theory."

SWM and stakeholder theory are not mutually exclusive. If managers are maximizing shareholder wealth, then many other stakeholder goals should be met as a natural consequence, and vice versa.

From a social welfare standpoint, however, it has been argued that SWM is superior to stakeholder theory. That is because SWM provides a single goal with explicit tradeoffs (i.e., spend an additional dollar on any constituency to the extent that this expenditure is expected to add a dollar or more to long-term firm value), whereas stakeholder theory admits/increases agency costs by allowing managers to support pet projects without regard to value creation (Jensen, 2002).

Note that although SWM provides a scorecard, it does not provide a vision/strategy (Jensen, 2002). For example, SWM does not tell a line worker in an automobile plant how to create value. Instead, this value creation requires that management structures be put in place that make day-to-day strategy clear, perhaps informed by stakeholder theory. Finally, note that none of these considerations require that value be easily observable or measurable: Intelligent management should recognize value creation.

Chapter 2

Financial Statements

I discuss briefly only the balance sheet (also called the "statement of financial position") and the income statement (also called the "revenue statement" or the "profit and loss statement"). Let me pick out three key concepts that commonly cause confusion.

First, the balance sheet stores a snapshot of the level of historical cost information. On the left hand side is the accumulated assets of the firm. On the right hand side is a summation of the owners' equity and liabilities. It is called a balance sheet because our accounting system balances all entries in such a way that the assets are balanced by the sum of equity and liabilities.

Note that sometimes, especially when discussing capital market implications, we will discuss a theoretical "market value balance sheet." In this case, the assets, liabilities, and equity are recorded at fair market values, rather than historical cost.

The income statement tells a story about, say, a year's worth of revenue and expenses. So, unlike the snapshot of levels recorded in the balance sheet, the income statement is like a movie or a flow. That is, the balance sheet carries a snapshot taken at a single date, but the income statement carries flows between two dates (i.e., the beginning of the period and the end of the period).

Second, the income statement and balance sheet feed into each other. The business was started at some time in the past with some initial assets, equity, and liabilities. After that, however, time passes and expenses are offset against revenues, taxes are paid on profits, dividends may have been paid, and the retained earnings are added to the owners' equity on the balance sheet. So, although we think of the balance sheet as a snapshot of a level at one point in time, it gets to that stage partly as a result of the accumulation of a time series of outputs from the income statements.

It flows the other way also. For example, if the firm pays cash to purchase a fixed asset, then total assets do not change, and no immediate transaction goes through the income statement. As the fixed asset is depreciated, however, the firm deducts a slice of that asset's cost as a charge against revenues over each of the coming years, reducing the net value of the asset in the balance sheet, and using the depreciation expense to reduce both future income and future taxes payable in the income statement.

Third, a big slice of the class deals with capital budgeting. There are many components to capital budgeting, each of equal importance, but one of the most difficult concepts for students to master (other than by memorization) is the construction of the FCFs (Chapter 9) that we feed into the capital budgeting decision rules (Chapter 8).

Related to this, it is important to realize that the income statement is built for *accounting* purposes but we need cash flow numbers for *valuation* purposes. For example, the income statement includes depreciation of physical assets and perhaps amortization of intangible assets, but neither of these is a cash expense. Similarly, the income statement deducts financing expenses like interest on debt, but that is a payment to a supplier of capital. So, it should not be subtracted when trying to figure cash flows available to suppliers of capital (rather, it *is* a cash flow to a supplier of capital; see Chapter 9). So, we need to unwind some accounting entries when calculating cash flows for valuation purposes.

Some financial analysts calculate earnings before interest, taxes, depreciation, and amortization (EBITDA; pronounced *ee-bit-dah*) to take out the effects of financing, taxes, and non-cash expenses.[1] EBITDA is a "bottom up" calculation on the income statement, working from the net income number at the bottom of the income statement and unwinding it until you get to EBITDA. That is, you start with the net income figure at the bottom (i.e., revenue less all expenses, less income tax), then you unwind, or peel back, the layers of accounting entries to get to the underlying finance.

Instead of using EBITDA, however, in Chapter 9 we calculate operating cash flow (OCF) as one component of FCF. OCF is calculated using a "top down" approach where you start with revenues and

---

[1]Note that abbreviations that I use repeatedly or without definition are listed starting on p. 237.

work down the income statement until you get to OCF.

OCF and EBITDA are similar in that they are both trying to get to the heart of the cash flows generated by the assets of the company, but EBITDA is before taxes (that is, it adds them back in as if they were never paid), and OCF is after taxes.

Note that OCF is going to feed into a valuation formula where we discount the after-tax FCFs using an after-tax discount rate. EBITDA is not typically used in this way. Rather, EBITDA is used by financial analysts in ratio analysis with comparable companies. So, EBITDA is for relative valuation, whereas OCF is for absolute valuation.

We will return to OCF in Chapter 9, where OCF feeds into the numerator in our discounted cash flow (DCF) analysis. Before we can do this, however, we need to discuss time value of money concepts.

Chapter 3

TVM I: One CF

The key idea in DCF analysis is that we must adjust cash flows "for changes in the value of money itself" (Williams, 1938, p. 55). The way in which the value of money changes through time depends upon the level of interest rates (including inflation), the riskiness of the cash flows generated by the project (Williams, 1938; Burrell, 1960), and, if we are using the CAPM, the market risk premium. Collectively, these determine the time-varying value of money, or just the "time value of money" (TVM).

You Need to Know: Percent

"Five percent" and "5%" and "0.05" are exactly the same thing and may be used interchangeably.

$$5\% = \text{five percent}$$
$$= \text{five per cent}$$
$$= 5 \text{ per cent}$$
$$= \frac{5}{\text{cent}} = \frac{5}{100} = 0.05,$$

where I replaced "cent" with "100." (How many years are there in a century, or cents in a dollar?)

Look at the % symbol. It is a line with a zero on either side. The line means divide by some denominator, and the two zeroes refer to how many zeroes go after the 1 in the denominator. That is, divide by 100. Some financial calculators even have a % key and pressing it simply divides by 100.

When we deal with very small numbers, for example, 0.05%, you can avoid getting confused by remembering that the % symbol means divide by 100. So, $0.05\% = 0.05 \div 100 = 0.0005$, which is 5 "basis points." (Note: 1%=100 basis points.)

Note that every interest rate must be accompanied by a term to be meaningful (e.g., 5% *per annum*).

In this chapter we look at TVM for a single cash flow. (Note that I sometimes abbreviate "cash flow" as "CF.") In the next chapter we introduce TVM for multiple cash flows.

Suppose you deposit \$100 in the bank at an interest rate of 5% for one year. Assume your tax rate on interest income is 20%. Then at the end of the year, you have \$105, and your bank will most likely deduct \$1 in taxes to send to the tax authority, leaving you with \$104. In this case, you earned 5% per annum before taxes, and 4% per annum after taxes. For our simple TVM examples from now on, however, we will ignore taxes (or assume all interest rates are after taxes). Taxes do not add to our understanding of TVM. We bring taxes back into the picture again later when we look at FCFs and discount rates for capital budgeting.

Ignoring taxes, in our previous example, the future value (FV) one year from now of our \$100 deposit is \$105, as represented by Equation 3.1.

$$
\begin{aligned}
FV &= PV \times (1 + r) \quad\quad (3.1) \\
&= \$100 \times (1.05) \\
&= \$105,
\end{aligned}
$$

where $PV = \$100$ is the present value and $r = 5\% = 0.05$ per annum.

Suppose we had invested our original $100 at 5% per annum for *two* years. Well, banks offer two types of interest on investments: simple interest and compound interest.

If the two-year investment earns *simple* interest of 5% per annum, then the bank credits you with $5 at the end of year one, and another $5 at the end of year two. So, the final balance (FB) is given by Equation 3.2.

$$
\begin{aligned}
FB &= PV \times [1 + (r \times 2)] \qquad (3.2) \\
&= \$100 \times [1 + (0.05 \times 2)] \\
&= \$100 \times (1.10) \\
&= \$110,
\end{aligned}
$$

where $PV = \$100$, $r = 5\% = 0.05$, and $t = 2$.

A more general formula for the future balance of a t-year deposit earning simple interest at rate r per annum is given in Equation 3.3.

$$
FB = PV \times [1 + (r \times t)] \qquad (3.3)
$$

If, however, the two-year investment earns *compound* interest of 5% per annum, then the bank credits you with $5 at the end of year one, and they then calculate interest at a rate of 5% upon the intermediate balance of $105. So, the future value is given by Equation 3.4. (See Figure 3.1 on p. 30.)

$$FV = PV \times (1+r) \times (1+r) \quad (3.4)$$
$$= \$100 \times (1+r)^2$$
$$= \$100 \times (1.05)^2$$
$$= \$110.25,$$

where $PV = \$100$ and $r = 5\% = 0.05$ per annum.[1]

A more general formula for the future value, FV, of a t-year deposit earning compound interest at rate r per annum is given in Equation 3.5.

$$FV = PV \times (1+r)^t \quad (3.5)$$

Let me make several points. First, the extra $0.25 earned in the compound interest example over and above the interest earned in the simple interest example is generated because you earned 5% interest during the second year on the $5 interest that arrives at the end of the first year.

---

[1] A+ students should be asking why any investor would deposit money for multiple years at one bank earning *simple* interest at 5% if that bank, or another bank, offers competing *compound* interest at 5%. One answer is that simple interest (assuming the interest is able to be withdrawn) may meet the intermediate cash flow income needs of some customers better than compound interest (where the interest is tied up for the long term). For some customers, this benefit may offset the loss of the interest on the interest.

Second, although the $0.25 "interest on your interest" seems insignificant, in long-term examples or if the interest rate is very high, the interest on the interest grows so strongly that it outweighs the simple interest by a large factor. For example, please use Equation 3.3 and Equation 3.5 to show that if $t = 50$ years, and $r = 0.10$ per annum, then $FV/FB \approx 19.57$ for any non-zero PV. That is, in this case your final wealth with compound interest is 19.57 times your final wealth with simple interest, driven by the interest on your interest.

Third, I used the "$\times$" symbol repeatedly in the above examples for multiplication. This symbol is usually omitted by financial economists because in more complex formulas it would appear so many times that it would obscure what is going on. So, I am going to stop using it now for the most part. For example, I will just write $FV = PV(1 + r)^t$.

Fourth, although banks certainly do offer simple interest products, most of the financial world operates using compound interest. So, when we calculate future values, we will almost always assume that there is compound interest, and we will use Equation 3.5 rather than Equation 3.3. In fact, I used the unusual notation FB to distinguish the unusual simple interest case from the more commonly used FV in the compound interest case.

Moving on, my experience with thousands of students is that they are much less likely to make an error in a TVM calculation if they draw a "timeline" and label it before solving a TVM problem. It is not quite so important in simple one- or two-period cases, but I have nevertheless drawn Figure 3.1 to illustrate the earning of the interest on the interest in our two-period case. Usually, however, we will be solving a more complex problem for an unknown quantity that is marked with a question mark, as we will see in Figures 3.2–3.4. I will discuss safe strategies for solving numerical problems shortly.

Our TVM I formula Equation 3.5 may be manipulated algebraically to solve for any one of the four components in terms of the others. These four different (but mathematically identical) ways to write Equation 3.5 are shown in Equations 3.6. (If you have difficulty with algebra, please see the note on the "dinner party rule" on p. 31.)

$$
\left.
\begin{array}{rrcl}
\text{How much (future)?} & FV & = & PV(1+r)^t \\[4pt]
\text{How much (present)?} & PV & = & \frac{FV}{(1+r)^t} \\[4pt]
\text{What rate?} & r & = & \left(\frac{FV}{PV}\right)^{\frac{1}{t}} - 1 \\[4pt]
\text{When?} & t & = & \frac{log_e\left(\frac{FV}{PV}\right)}{log_e(1+r)}
\end{array}
\right\}
\tag{3.6}
$$

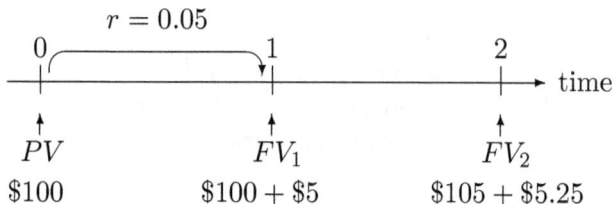

Figure 3.1: Two-Period Compound Interest

You invest initial principal of $100 at $t = 0$. The interest rate is 5% per annum for two years. (Note that I indicate the interest on my timelines only for the first period.) After one year, your $100 principal generates $5 in interest. The new principal of $105 then generates additional interest of $5.25 at the end of the second year. You can also view the $5.25 as $5 of interest on the intermediate (i.e., $t = 1$) $100 principal plus another $0.25 interest on the intermediate $5 interest. Thus, FV_2 is what you would earn with simple interest of 5% per annum plus a boost from the interest on the interest. Note that usually our timelines will have an unknown quantity on them (e.g., PV, FV, t or r) that we are aiming to solve for. I usually indicate the unknown with a question mark.

You Need to Know: Dinner Party Rule

How do I get from $FV = PV(1 + r)^t$ to, say, $r = \left(\frac{FV}{PV}\right)^{\frac{1}{t}} - 1$ in Equations 3.6?

At a fancy dinner party, you will find multiple pieces of cutlery laid to either side of your plate. What to do? The basic rule of etiquette is that you use the outermost pair of cutlery for the first course, then the next pair for the second course, etc. That is, you work from the outside in.

Applying the dinner party rule here, starting with $FV = PV(1 + r)^t$, you solve for r by working from the outside of the RHS in towards the target r, removing variables as you go. As long as you start with an equality (i.e., LHS=RHS), and perform valid operations on both sides of the equals sign, you will still have an equality.

$$FV = PV(1 + r)^t \text{ (}\div \text{ both sides by PV)}$$

$$\frac{FV}{PV} = (1 + r)^t \text{ (raise both sides to } 1/t)$$

$$\left(\frac{FV}{PV}\right)^{\frac{1}{t}} = (1 + r) \text{ (subtract 1 from both sides)}$$

$$\left(\frac{FV}{PV}\right)^{\frac{1}{t}} - 1 = r \text{ (swap sides and you are done)}$$

A Note on Logarithms

One line of Equations 3.6 uses logarithms to state that $t = \frac{log_e\left(\frac{FV}{PV}\right)}{log_e(1+r)}$. If you struggle with mathematics and do not plan to major in finance, there is little harm in viewing the logarithm function as a black-box transformation that you do not need to understand. That is, if you want to find $log_e(1 + r)$ for $r = 0.05$, say, then find the log_e button on your calculator (it may be labeled ln) and simply evaluate it at 1.05.

For A+ students, many books (e.g., Crack, 2017a) or Web pages discuss details of logarithms. Note that if you begin with $FV = PV(1 + r)^t$ and use the dinner party rule from p. 31, you get $t = \frac{log_b\left(\frac{FV}{PV}\right)}{log_b(1+r)}$ for arbitrary base $b > 0$, $b \neq 1$. I presented it using natural logarithms (i.e., $b = e$) only because that is a simple/common choice.

If you are an ace student, then you can go further:

$$t = \frac{log_b\left(\frac{FV}{PV}\right)}{log_b(1+r)} = log_{(1+r)}\left(\frac{FV}{PV}\right),$$

doing away with the arbitrary logarithmic base entirely. Most handheld calculators cannot, however, handle logarithmic bases other than 10 and e.

Two Notes on Handheld Calculators

With handheld calculators, always guess the answer before doing the calculation! For example, what is the FV of $100 invested at 5% per annum for 10 years? The simple interest is $5 per year, bringing the FV to at least $150. Compound interest increases the FV, but the FV is probably not as high as $200, because the term is so short. Now check my guess of $150 \leq FV \leq$ $200.

Many students, however, view their handheld calculator as some sort of oracle. So, they hammer numbers into it carelessly and get complete garbage out, which they then record as their answer, devoid of any intuition. For example, they might tell me that $100 growing at 5% per annum for 10 years grows to be worth $-$26,532.98, when clearly they just hit the wrong key(s). How could the answer be negative or that big? Having a guess first means that a terrible answer will stand out as terrible, and you will then repeat the calculation more carefully.

Finally, I own five fancy financial calculators made by HP. I love them, but I strongly recommend that my students use only a basic scientific calculator. Complicated financial calculators confuse students and interfere with their learning/understanding.

Let us do some examples to illustrate the use of timelines and safe strategies for solving our numerical problems. After grading many thousands of student answers, I can tell you that these strategies frame the problem, increase your chance of getting the correct answer, and increase the chance for partial credit.

TVM I: Solve for *PV*

Suppose you want to have $500 in your savings account two years from now. Suppose the bank offers a 4% interest rate after all taxes and fees. How much do you need to deposit now? The first thing to do is draw the timeline as in Figure 3.2. The

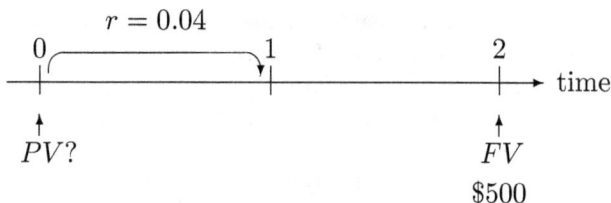

Figure 3.2: TVM I Example: Solve for *PV*

next thing to do is have a guess. With $r > 0$, *PV* must be less than $FV = \$500$. If I squint, 4% for two years is about 10% in total. So, I will guess

PV is about 10% less than \$500, which would give $PV \approx \$450$.

Next, I pick an equation to use. Because only a single cash flow is involved (i.e., the \$500 at $t = 2$), I choose one of the four lines from Equations 3.6. I wish to solve for PV, so I choose $PV = FV/(1+r)^t$.

Next, I write out the formula algebraically and also with the numbers plugged in:

$$PV = \frac{FV}{(1+r)^t} = \frac{\$500}{(1.04)^2}.$$

Then I evaluate it using my calculator to get $PV = \$462.28$ (rounding to the nearest penny here).

Next, I compare my answer with my guess; it is in the ball park, so there are no red flags.

Finally, there is often a way to double-check your answer using a simpler formula (i.e., one less likely to lead you to an error). In this case, the simplest TVM I formula is $FV = PV(1+r)^t$. If I plug my answer for PV into it (keeping all the decimal places in my calculator) along with $r = 0.04$ and $t = 2$, do I get the \$500 future value I am supposed to get? Yes, I do!

TVM I: Solve for r

Suppose you have \$200 to invest at $t = 0$ for four

years. Suppose you want to double your money. What interest rate would you have to earn per annum? The first thing to do is draw the timeline as in Figure 3.3. The next thing to do is have a guess.

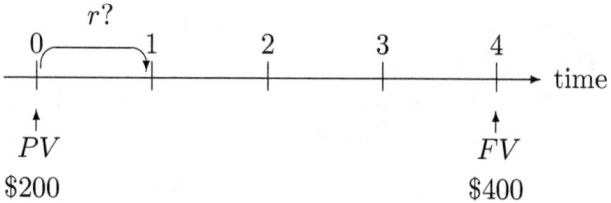

Figure 3.3: TVM I Example: Solve for r

Well, to double my money in four years using *simple* interest instead of compound interest, I need to earn a total of \$200 in interest. That equates to \$50 simple interest per annum. That is, a simple interest rate of $r = 0.25$ per annum. The benefits of compounding mean my answer will be less than 25% per annum. My guess is that an interest rate of around $r = 20\%$ per annum will work.

Next, I pick an equation to use. Because only a single cash flow is involved (i.e., with PV of \$200 at $t = 0$ or with FV of \$400 at $t = 4$), I choose one of the lines from Equations 3.6. I wish to solve for r, so I choose $r = \left(\frac{FV}{PV}\right)^{\frac{1}{t}} - 1$.

Next, I write out the formula algebraically and also with the numbers plugged in:

$$r = \left(\frac{FV}{PV}\right)^{\frac{1}{t}} - 1 = \left(\frac{400}{200}\right)^{\frac{1}{4}} - 1.$$

Then I evaluate it using my calculator to get $r = 0.1892$ per annum (rounding to four decimal places here). That is 18.92% per annum.

Next, I compare my answer with my guess; it is in the ball park, so, there are no red flags.

Finally, I want to double-check my answer using a simpler formula. Again, the simplest TVM I formula is $FV = PV(1 + r)^t$. If I plug my answer for r into it (keeping all the decimal places in my calculator), along with $PV = \$200$ and $t = 4$, do I get the \$400 future value I am supposed to get? Yes, I do!

TVM I: Solve for t

Suppose you have \$1,000 to invest at $t = 0$. Suppose you can earn 8% per annum. How long until you have \$3,000? Again, the first thing to do is to draw the timeline as in Figure 3.4. The next thing to do is have a guess. Well, at 8% per annum, you make \$80 in the first year. I'll squint and call that \$100. At that rate, it will take 20 years to earn the \$2,000

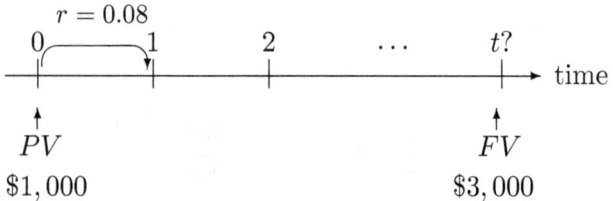

Figure 3.4: TVM I Example: Solve for t

interest needed to bring your balance up to the FV of \$3,000. I figure that compounding will help me out by reducing the term. So, my ball-park guess is something like 15 years.

Next, I pick an equation to use. Because only a single cash flow is involved (i.e., the \$1,000 at $t = 0$ or the \$3,000 at t), I choose one of the lines from Equations 3.6. I wish to solve for t, so I choose $t = log_e\left(\frac{FV}{PV}\right)/log_e(1 + r)$.

Next, I write out the formula algebraically and also with the numbers plugged in:

$$t = \frac{log_e\left(\frac{FV}{PV}\right)}{log_e(1 + r)} = \frac{log_e\left(\frac{3,000}{1,000}\right)}{log_e(1.08)} = \frac{log_e(3)}{log_e(1.08)}.$$

Then I evaluate it using my calculator to get $t = 14.2749$ years (rounding to four decimal places).

Next, I compare my answer with my guess; it is

in the ball park again, so, there are no red flags and
no obvious need to re-compute.

Finally, I want to check my answer using a
simpler formula. The simplest TVM I formula is
$FV = PV(1 + r)^t$. If I plug my answer for t into it
(keeping all the decimal places in my calculator),
along with $PV = \$1,000$ and $r = 0.08$, do I get the
$FV = \$3,000$ answer I expect? Yes, I do!

TVM I: Summary of Safe Strategies

- Draw a time line. Label it with what you know,
  and put a question mark beside the unknown
  quantity you seek.

- Have a rough guess at the answer you expect.

- Write down the formula you plan to use, with
  algebraic symbols.

- Then write down the formula with the numbers
  filled in.

- Perform the calculation and confirm that your
  guess is in the ball park. Repeat your calculation
  if the answer is far from your guess.

- Try to double-check your answer by plugging it
  back into a simpler formula.

Chapter 4

TVM II: Multiple CFs

In Chapter 3 we looked only at a single cash flow and its PV, FV, implied interest rate r, or required investment horizon t. In the real world, contracts involving multiple cash flows are, however, much more common than contracts involving a single cash flow. For example, you buy a TV and pay it off with monthly cash flows over three years, or you start a job and you deposit 10% of your income each month to a retirement savings scheme until you retire, or you borrow money to buy a house, and you pay the loan back monthly over 20 years.

Why would you be interested in the *FV* of the deposits to a retirement savings scheme, or the *PV* of the repayments to a mortgage loan? Well, in the case of the retirement savings scheme, the *FV* of the deposits, if calculated at your proposed retirement date, is your projected lump sum balance at retirement. This value will help to determine whether you can retire with enough assets to stop work if you wish, travel, meet healthcare costs, etc. In the case of the repayments on the mortgage loan, the general rule of thumb is that the *PV* of the repayments equals the amount of the initial loan. So, in order to calculate how much you can borrow (and thus how much of a house you can afford), a bank will first figure out how much you can afford to pay back each month. They then discount those repayments to figure out how much they can lend you.

So, figuring out TVM calculations with multiple cash flow contracts is important. That is what most of this chapter is about. Unfortunately, dealing with multiple cash flow TVM calculations has been the single most common source of errors in exams for students in this class.

Let me begin by pointing out a ridiculous error. Given dozens of cash flows through time, sure enough their *PV* or *FV* can be calculated by adding up the results of repeated application of the single-cash-flow techniques from Chapter 3. Indeed, some of my students who skipped classes end up doing exactly this on the final exam. It is nearly impossible, however, to discount dozens of cash flows individually by hand, add them up, and get the correct answer. There are too many opportunities to get the answer wrong. Even if students do manage to get a numerically correct answer, I will still deduct marks for their ignorance of the superior techniques.

So, the first lesson to learn here is that when presented with multiple cash flows that have the pattern of an annuity (i.e., a finite series of equal-sized cash flows regularly spaced in time) or a perpetuity (i.e., an infinite series of equal-sized cash flows regularly spaced in time), a mental light bulb should flash immediately telling you that it is time to use an annuity or perpetuity formula—a single formula that solves a complicated problem for you in one go. So, you must always be on the lookout for these regular cash flow patterns.

TVM II: Ordinary Annuity Algebra

Figure 4.1 shows an ordinary annuity of N cash flows. They are equally spaced in time and each is for amount C. For example, it might be $N =$

240 monthly cash flows each of \$1,400 to repay a mortgage over 20 years.

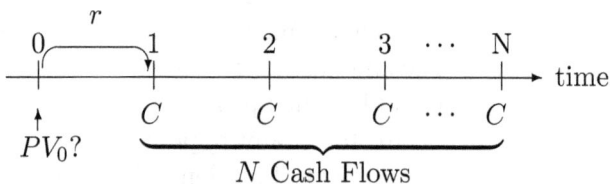

Figure 4.1: TVM II Algebra: Ordinary Annuity

Question: What is it about the equal-sized cash flows in Figure 4.1 that makes the cash flow pattern an *ordinary* annuity rather than an annuity *due*? **Answer:** It is only the fact that we are going to find the *PV* one step prior to the first cash flow that makes it an ordinary annuity.

We could use our TVM I mathematics to discount every individual flow in Figure 4.1 back to time $t = 0$. As mentioned previously, however, that would be both time consuming and prone to error.

---

[1]The *PV* is also given by, equivalently,

$$PV = C \frac{\left[1 - \frac{1}{(1+r)^N}\right]}{r} = \frac{C}{r}\left[1 - (1+r)^{-N}\right].$$

If we do it algebraically, however, and add them all up (have a go if you are good at algebra), it can be shown that the PV at time $t = 0$ of the annuity in Figure 4.1 is given by Equation 4.1.[1]

$$PV = \frac{C}{r}\left[1 - \frac{1}{(1+r)^N}\right] \qquad (4.1)$$

Before we do some examples, let me point out a tremendous source of confusion for students. Look at Figure 4.2 and ask yourself what is the PV_8 of the annuity in Figure 4.2?

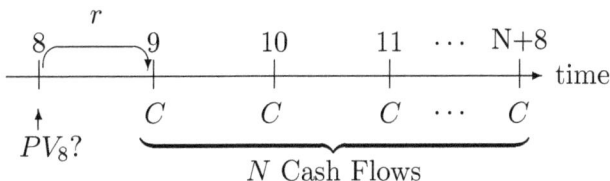

Figure 4.2: TVM II Algebra: Ordinary Annuity

Well, the PV_8 of the annuity in Figure 4.2 is *identical* to the PV_0 of the annuity in Figure 4.1. I changed the labels on the axis, but not the interest rates, nor the cash flow amount or frequency, nor the count of the cash flows. The labels on the timeline do not in any way determine the PV of an annuity of N cash flows calculated one step prior to the first cash flow. So, PV_8 in Figure 4.2 is the same as PV_0 in Figure 4.1 and is given by Equation 4.1.

TVM II: Solve for *PV* of Ordinary Annuity
You are standing at $t = 0$. You will pay 240 monthly cash flows starting one month from now. Each is \$1,400. The interest rate is $r = 0.0035$ per month (i.e., slightly more than one-third of a percentage point per month). What is the present value of the annuity?

As previously, start by drawing a timeline. Be sure to label it clearly (see Figure 4.3). Then guess the answer. Then choose the formula and write it out algebraically, and then with numbers. Then calculate the answer.

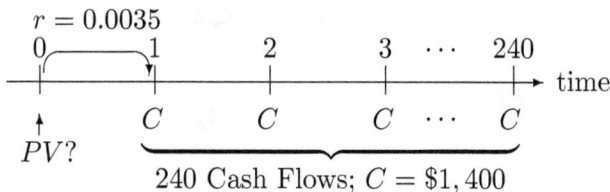

Figure 4.3: TVM II Example: Ordinary Annuity Solve for *PV*

I want to use Equation 4.1 for an ordinary annuity, but first I need to guess at the numerical answer. How can I guess the PV of 240 cash flows spaced over 20 years? Let us take an aside on perpetuities.

You Need to Know: Perpetuity

Beginning in 1751, the U.K. government was well known for <u>consol</u>idating its debts into bonds that paid perpetual coupons. The last of these "consol" bonds (also called "undated gilts") was redeemed in July 2015 (DMO, 2017).

Suppose you receive a cash flow C starting one period from now and another cash flow C every period thereafter in perpetuity. What is the present value of this cash flow stream?

If you are good at mathematics, some algebra quickly shows that the PV of the perpetuity is given by Equation 4.2.

$$PV = \frac{C}{r} \qquad (4.2)$$

It makes sense that there is no count of cash flows in the formula, because the count is infinite. Alternatively, if you let $N \to \infty$ in Equation 4.1, you arrive at Equation 4.2 for any $r > 0$.

Well, an annuity of 240 payments of \$1,400 cannot be worth more than the analogous perpetuity (because the perpetuity has all the same cash flows as the annuity plus an extra tail of cash flows at the end). So, I can put an upper bound on the PV of the annuity using the PV of the perpetuity:

$$PV(\text{annuity}) \leq C/r = \$1,400/0.0035 = \$400,000.$$

If I find a PV number larger than this outcome, then it must be wrong. I am not, however, immediately sure how much smaller than this my annuity's PV will be. (The higher the interest rate, the smaller the value of the distant tail of cash flows, but $r = 0.0035$ per month is not a very large rate.)

Now we use Equation 4.1.

$$
\begin{aligned}
PV &= \frac{C}{r}\left[1 - \frac{1}{(1+r)^N}\right] \\
&\quad \frac{\$1,400}{0.0035}\left[1 - \frac{1}{(1.0035)^{240}}\right] \\
&= \$227,062.32
\end{aligned}
$$

The answer is below my upper bound with no obvious red flags. There is no obviously simpler formula to check it with in this case.

TVM II: *FV* of Ordinary Annuity

I can plug Equation 4.1 into Equation 3.5 with

$t = N$ to deduce that the FV of the ordinary annuity at the date of the last cash flow is given by Equation 4.3.

$$
\begin{aligned}
FV &= PV(1+r)^N \\
&= \left\{ \frac{C}{r} \left[1 - \frac{1}{(1+r)^N} \right] \right\} (1+r)^N \\
&= \frac{C}{r} \left[(1+r)^N - 1 \right] \quad (4.3)
\end{aligned}
$$

TVM II: Ordinary Annuity Solve for N

I can apply the dinner party rule (see p. 31) to Equation 4.1 and Equation 4.3, to deduce N (i.e., the number of cash flows) in terms of either the PV or the FV of the ordinary annuity, respectively, as shown in Equation 4.4.[2]

$$
N = \frac{log_e \left[\frac{C}{C - r \times PV} \right]}{log_e (1+r)} = \frac{log_e \left[1 + \frac{r \times FV}{C} \right]}{log_e (1+r)} \quad (4.4)
$$

For example, how many monthly cash flows of $1,000 are needed to repay a borrowing of $PV = $50,000$ if the interest rate is $r = 0.0050$ (i.e., half a percentage point) per month?

---

[2]A+ students should note that I have again used natural logarithms, but that these results are true for $log_b(\cdot)$ for any base $b > 0$, $b \neq 1$.

The first step of our safe strategy to solve TVM problems is to sketch a timeline, as in Figure 4.4. The next step is to have a guess. If the interest rate

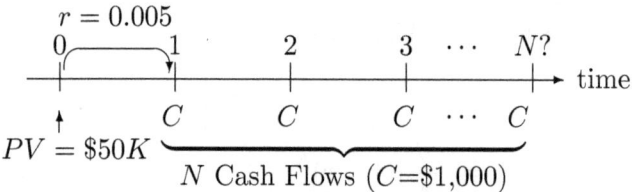

Figure 4.4: TVM II Example: Ordinary Annuity Solve for N

is zero, it would take $N = 50$ cash flows to repay the loan. With $r > 0$, it must take more than 50 cash flows, but given how low the interest rate is, it is probably not going to be very many more.

The next step is to write out the equation algebraically, and plug the numbers in, as follows:

$$N = \frac{log_e\left[\frac{C}{C - r \times PV}\right]}{log_e(1 + r)}$$

$$= \frac{log_e\left[\frac{\$1,000}{\$1,000 - 0.005 \times \$50,000}\right]}{log_e(1.005)}$$

$$= \frac{log_e(1.33\dot{3})}{log_e(1.005)} = 57.68 \text{ months,}$$

to two decimal places. This answer is close to my ball-park guess. So, now I want to check it using a simpler formula, preferably without logarithms. If I use the PV of an ordinary annuity formula (Equation 4.1) with $C = \$1,000$, $r = 0.005$ per month, and $N = 57.68$ (be sure to keep all the decimal places in your calculator), do I get back $PV = \$50,000$? Yes, it works exactly!

Note that in this last example, the answer for N is not a whole number. There is no mathematical reason why the complicated formula in Equation 4.4 should return a whole number. In practice, of course, any bank lending you money will offer repayments spread over a whole number of months. In that case, however, fixing a rounded N means that the repayment itself is unlikely to be a round number (see the following example).

TVM II: Ordinary Annuity Solve for C

Can you solve for the value of C that repays a $\$50,000$ loan in, say, 60 months, at a rate of $r = 0.005$ per month? Assume an ordinary annuity.

The first step of our safe strategy is to draw a timeline as in Figure 4.5. The next step is to have a guess. We know from the previous example that when paying back $\$1,000$ per month it takes just

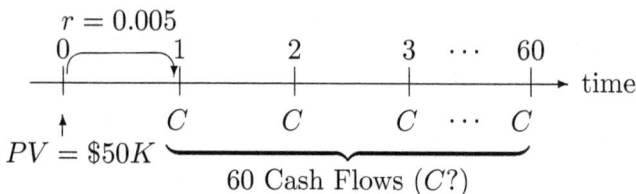

Figure 4.5: TVM II Example: Ordinary Annuity Solve for C

over 57 months to extinguish the $50,000 debt. If we take a little longer (i.e., 60 months) to pay back the same debt, then the payment per month will be a little lower. I am going to guess that C is somewhere between $950 and $1,000 per month.

The next thing to do is to take the formula for the PV of an annuity (Equation 4.1) and use the dinner party rule (p. 31) to rearrange the formula to get a formula for C as in Equation 4.5 (exercise: check that you can derive this formula).

$$C = \frac{PV}{\frac{1}{r}\left[1 - \frac{1}{(1+r)^N}\right]} \qquad (4.5)$$

Next we plug the values in as shown in Equation 4.6.

$$C = \frac{\$50,000}{\frac{1}{0.005}\left[1 - \frac{1}{(1.005)^{60}}\right]} = \$966.64, \qquad (4.6)$$

to the nearest penny—within my ballpark range.

Finally, we check the solution with a simpler formula. If I plug $C = \$966.64$ (keeping all the decimal places from my calculator), $N = 60$ and $r = 0.005$, back into the PV of the ordinary annuity (Equation 4.1), do I get back \$50,000? Yes, I do!

Note that in Chapter 3, we solved Equation 3.5 (i.e., TVM I) for each of FV, PV, r, and t (see Equations 3.6 on p. 29). We just solved Equation 4.1 for PV, FV, N, and C, but we will not be solving for r. That is because Equation 4.1 is typically too complex to solve *explicitly* in terms of r, requiring a trial and error approach instead.

Job Interview Question: You are seated at a table that has 100 quarters on it. Unfortunately, the room is pitch black and you cannot see the quarters. You also cannot tell by touch which way up they are, but you are told that there are 10 heads and 90 tails turned up. How can you divide them into two piles where you have the same number of heads in each pile?

Taken from *Heard on The Street: Quantitative Questions from Wall Street Job Interviews*,
©2017 Timothy Falcon Crack. See advertisements at the end of this book.

Note on PV of an Ordinary Annuity

You should note that an ordinary annuity is just a perpetuity with its tail cut off. That is, standing at time $t = 0$, receiving N cash flows each of C starting at $t = 1$, is like receiving the income from being long (i.e., buying) a perpetuity of cash flows C starting at $t = 1$, and being "short" (i.e., selling off) a perpetuity of cash flows C starting at $t = N + 1$.

So, the PV of the ordinary annuity should be plus the PV of a perpetuity (i.e., $+ C/r$), minus the value at $t = 0$ of a perpetuity whose first cash flow is at $t = N + 1$. The latter perpetuity has value C/r at time $t = N$, and therefore value $C/r \times 1/(1+r)^N$ at time $t = 0$.

So, the PV of the ordinary annuity must be

$$
\begin{aligned}
PV &= + \frac{C}{r} - \left[\frac{C}{r} \times \frac{1}{(1+r)^N} \right] \\
&= \frac{C}{r} \left[1 - \frac{1}{(1+r)^N} \right],
\end{aligned}
$$

as given already in Equation 4.1.

Another Note on Handheld Calculators

Complicated TVM formulas often have intermediate calculations that you need to feed into later calculations. Students who do not keep all the decimal places in intermediate calculations typically lose marks for failing to do so. Sometimes you can enter the intermediate calculations into your calculator using parentheses, but I often use the memory in my calculator instead.

Most modern handheld calculators have multiple memories. That is, there will be, say, Memory #1, ..., Memory #5, or Memory A, ..., Memory E, or similar. If you can master the use of the memories, then you have places to store multiple intermediate calculations.

When I place an intermediate calculation in a memory I often write on my page a little "1" or "A", or whatever, in a small circle beside the intermediate calculation to indicate which memory to retrieve that number from when I need it. The circle signals that my note is not part of the formula.

You can use an Internet search engine to search for the manual for your model of calculator to figure out how to master its memories.

TVM II: *PV* of Annuity Due

In my experience, most students simply do not understand the "annuity due" concept. Look at the timeline in Figure 4.6. We know the *PV* of the an-

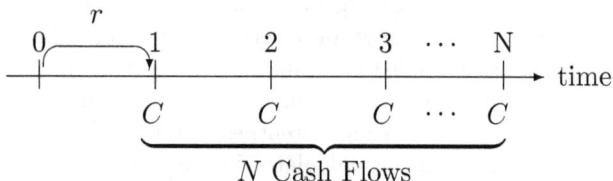

Figure 4.6: TVM II Algebra: Annuity Time Line

nuity at $t = 0$ is given by Equation 4.1. In that case, we refer to the annuity as an "ordinary annuity." I could, however, have asked you to value the annuity at any point on the timeline (e.g., $t = 0$, or $t = 1$, or $t = 2$, ..., or $t = N$, or $t = N + 1$, etc.).

Now look back at the TVM I formula in Equation 3.5 (see p. 27). If I know the *PV* of the annuity in Figure 4.6 at $t = 0$, then I can find its *FV* at any point t on the timeline by plugging Equation 4.1 into Equation 3.5 as shown in Equation 4.7.

$$
\begin{aligned}
FV_t &= PV_0 \times (1 + r)^t \\
&= \left\{ \frac{C}{r} \left[1 - \frac{1}{(1 + r)^N} \right] \right\} \times (1 + r)^t \quad (4.7)
\end{aligned}
$$

In the special case where I plug $t = N$ into Equation 4.7, I can do a little tidying up of terms, to arrive at the FV of the ordinary annuity at the date of the final cash flow of the annuity—the same as the formula in Equation 4.3 as stated on p. 49.

In the special case where I plug $t = 1$ into Equation 4.7, I get the FV of the ordinary annuity at the date of its first cash flow. This is an interesting case. In practice, some annuities begin immediately. That is, their first cash flow is already due. Such an annuity is referred to as an *annuity due*. If you are standing at $t = 0$ in Figure 4.6, then the annuity looks like an ordinary annuity, with its first cash flow one period hence. If, however, you are standing at $t = 1$ in Figure 4.6, then the annuity is an annuity due, with its first cash flow already due. Plugging $t = 1$ into Equation 4.7, yields Equation 4.8 for the PV of an annuity due.

$$PV = \frac{C}{r} \left[1 - \frac{1}{(1+r)^N} \right] (1+r) \qquad (4.8)$$

That is, all I did to find the PV of the annuity due was to find its PV at $t = 0$ (i.e., the value of an ordinary annuity), and then use TVM I math to compound it ahead in time by one period.

Most Common Annuity Mistake: $N =$ Count

I asked you previously to compare the *PV* of the annuities in Figure 4.1 and Figure 4.2. One reason I asked this is that the most common mistake students make with annuities is to use the wrong number for N in annuity formulas (e.g., Figure 4.2 with N versus $N + 8$).

Students will often just find the final cash flow in the annuity and read the number off the number line from beside that cash flow and enter that for N. This is nuts.

N in Equation 4.1 for the *PV* of an ordinary annuity is the *count* of the number of cash flows in the annuity. Oftentimes this count is different from the number on the timeline beside the final cash flow.

So, whether using an ordinary annuity formula or an annuity due formula, always *count* the number of cash flows, and enter that for N.

Some people use t in the annuity formula in place of my N, but I think that confuses students, because t is often used to denote *time* on the timeline. I chose N because I think it better signifies a *count*.

Most Common Annuity Mistake:
$N = $ Count (Addendum)

It is not just that many students misunderstand the role played by N in the formulas $PV = \frac{C}{r}\left[1 - \frac{1}{(1+r)^N}\right]$ (ordinary annuity) and $PV = \frac{C}{r}\left[1 - \frac{1}{(1+r)^N}\right](1 + r)$ (annuity due). Even students who know that N is the *count* of cash flows still often enter the wrong number for N.

Suppose today is Bob's 65th birthday. He has saved \$1,000,000 in his retirement account. Bob plans to withdraw the same amount C on every birthday starting today and ending 20 years from now on his 85th birthday. Bob earns 5% per annum in his account. How much is C? We will need to rearrange the annuity due formula to get C in terms of $PV = \$1M$, $r = 0.05$, and N.

Half my students will mistakenly use $N = 20$. A safe strategy is to make a mark with your pen (I use dots in groups of five) as you count in your head the birthdays: 65, 66, 67, 68, ..., 85. You should have marked $N = 21$ dots on your page.

Of course, you drew a timeline, took a guess, and checked your answer by plugging $C = \$74,282.01$ (do we agree?) back into Equation 4.8.

TVM II: *FV* of an Annuity Due

Look again at Figure 4.6. Standing at $t = 0$, the cash flows are an ordinary annuity (*PV* given in Equation 4.1). Standing at $t = 1$, the cash flows are an annuity due (*PV* given in Equation 4.8).

I already know the *FV* of an ordinary annuity at the date of its last cash flow. That was given by Equation 4.3 on p. 49: $FV = \frac{C}{r}\left[(1 + r)^N - 1\right]$.

Can you deduce immediately the *FV* of the annuity due on the date of its last cash flow?

Well, the simple fact of the matter is that the labels on the timeline are irrelevant. Let us remove them and redraw Figure 4.6 as Figure 4.7. Stand-

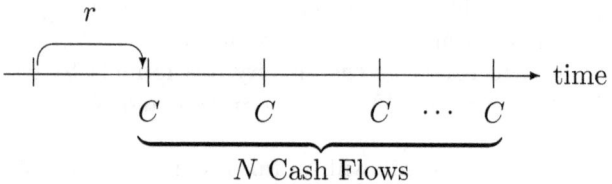

Figure 4.7: TVM II Algebra: Annuity Time Line

ing one step before the first cash flow, the cash flows are an ordinary annuity (*PV* given in Equation 4.1). Standing at the time of the first cash flow, the cash flows are an annuity due (*PV* given in Equation 4.8).

Standing at the date of the last cash flow in Figure 4.7, I cannot tell whether the annuity is an ordinary annuity of an annuity due—the cash flow timelines are the same. So, at the date of the last cash flow, the FV of the annuity due must be identical to the FV of the ordinary annuity: $FV = \frac{C}{r} \left[(1 + r)^N - 1 \right]$. Although there can be no other conclusion, this is a common source of confusion for students.

Note that some texts give the FV of the annuity due one period *after* its last cash flow. Compounding our last answer one period ahead gives this answer as $FV = \frac{C}{r} \left[(1 + r)^N - 1 \right] (1 + r)$.

Finally, note that handheld calculators often use numerical techniques to *estimate* TVM calculation answers when using large powers and compounding over many periods. Generally, though not always, the more expensive the calculator, the better the quality of the code being executed, and the more accurate the estimate. You may find with some cheap calculator models, however, that you are several pennies away from answers calculated by your friends who have more expensive calculators. Any instructor should allow for these numerical inaccuracies and not deduct marks.

A Growing Annuity

Any finance major aiming to ace the class should know that the *PV* formulas for the perpetuity and ordinary annuity in this chapter are special cases of a more general formula not usually shown to first-year finance students.

Consider an annuity of N cash flows starting one period from now. Let the first cash flow be C, and assume the cash flows grow at rate g per period, with discount rate $r > 0$ per period. Then the *PV* of this growing annuity is given in Equation 4.9.

$$PV = \frac{C}{r-g}\left[1 - \left(\frac{1+g}{1+r}\right)^N\right]$$

$$= \begin{cases} \frac{C}{r}, & \text{if } g = 0, \ N = \infty, \text{ and} \\[2mm] \frac{C}{(r-g)}, & \text{if } g < r, \ N = \infty, \text{ and} \\[2mm] \frac{C}{r}\left[1 - \left(\frac{1}{1+r}\right)^N\right], & \text{if } g = 0. \end{cases}$$

$$(4.9)$$

The first case is the perpetuity; the last is the ordinary annuity. The middle case appears as Equation 7.2 in Chapter 7, but with D_1 (a dividend) in place of C. Challenge: Use the logic in this chapter to figure out the *PV* of a growing annuity *due*.

TVM II: Summary of Key Concepts

- Always be on the lookout for annuities. Do not accidentally discount annuities term-by-term, because it is time consuming and error prone.[3]

- The amount of a loan is equal to the PV of the repayments on the loan (ignoring any additional administrative fees that might be charged). This is a key result that is often exploited to solve numerical problems.

- In any annuity formula, N is the *count* of the number of cash flows. Do not confuse N with any timeline label.

- More generally, the numerical labels on the timeline are not relevant for valuation. All that matters is the size of the cash flows, the count of the cash flows, the frequency (e.g., monthly, annually, etc.) of the cash flows, the discount rate, and the

---

[3]Note that in a complicated TVM problem, which may ask for the combined FV of multiple annuities and lump sums, it is almost always safest to discount all the cash flows back to time 0 initially (the PVs may then be added up and compounded forward to the required date). Students who use this time-0 approach make many fewer errors than those who compound component cash flows forward initially and then add them up.

timing of the valuation.

- An annuity is "ordinary" if you are valuing it one step prior to the first cash flow, but "due" if you are valuing it at the date of the first cash flow.

- The *FV* of an ordinary annuity and of an annuity due are identical if calculated at the date of the final cash flow.

- Learn to use the memories of your calculator to store intermediate answers, so as not to lose any decimal places. Losing decimal places can lead to a loss of marks.

- The same safe strategy rules given in Chapter 3 apply: draw a timeline, label it, have a guess, write down the formula algebraically, fill in the numbers, confirm that your answer is in the ball park, and double-check with a simpler formula where possible.

Chapter 5

Inflation and Indices

Inflation can be confusing. Let me walk through the most common sources of inflation-related mistakes by students in exams.[1]

Inflation is the change in the price of some real good or service. Oftentimes when folks talk about inflation they are referring to changes in the prices of a general basket of goods and services purchased by urban households. In the U.S., the Bureau of Labor Statistics (BLS) keeps track of this sort

---

[1]Graham (2006, pp. 47–64) has a nice discussion of inflation, both in general and from an investing perspective.

---

of inflation using the consumer price index (CPI). There are all sorts of problems and issues associated with the measurement of these general inflation rates. Discussion of these issues belongs in a high-level economics class, not a first finance class. The BLS produces several different time series of CPI numbers for slightly different purposes (BLS, 2015). The BLS also produces other inflation index measures that are less well known to the lay person.

In this class, we typically refer simply to the "rate of inflation." This rate is the change in the level of the CPI (or something like the CPI). For example, if the CPI index changes from 235.00 to 237.35 over the course of a year, then the rate of inflation that year is 1% (see also the box on p. 68.)

When we perform compounding or discounting at some required rate of return r, say, that discount rate r almost always includes inflation already. For example, suppose you go to the bank and they offer you a five-year certificate of deposit (CD) (i.e., they pay you interest for a fixed period of time but your money is not "on call," that is, you cannot withdraw the money until maturity). Suppose the bank offers you an interest rate of 4% per annum.

The quoted 4% number is a "nominal" rate of interest. That is, it is what you earn when counting the number of actual dollars received. For example, $1,000 deposited at 4% for one year is worth $1,040 at maturity before any taxes are subtracted.[2] Each $1 of those final 1,040 dollars will, however, likely buy fewer goods and services than each $1 of the initial 1,000 because of the effects of inflation.

The 4% rate of return is meant to compensate you for several different economic items. You need to be compensated for time preference (discussed in detail in Chapter 12). You also need to be compensated for anticipated inflation. For long-term deposits, you also need to be compensated for interest rate risk. That is, if your money is tied up for a long period of time earning a fixed interest rate, there is a chance that interest rates in general might rise, leaving you earning a below-market rate. So, you need a little extra boost in the rate offered to you to compensate you for exposure to that risk.

---

[2]My U.S. bank was offering one-year CD rates of only 1% in early 2016. In New Zealand (N.Z.), where interest rates are usually much higher than in the U.S., one-year CD rates were around 4%. Interest rates globally, even in N.Z., have been artificially depressed by central banks. The thinking is that more people are likely to invest in businesses when borrowing rates are low, thereby boosting economic growth. Conversely, higher interest rates can be used by central banks to fight inflation and slow down an overheated economy.

You Need to Know: Index Level and Rate

An "index" is the level of some economic quantity of interest. For example, the S&P 500 is an average of the prices of just over 500 stocks. The CPI in the U.S. is an average of the prices of about 200 consumer goods and services.

Often times, however, it is not the *level* of the index but the *rate of change* of level, expressed as a decimal or in percentage terms, that we are interested in. So, for example, if the S&P 500 index moves from 1,987.05 at the close of business Monday to 2,011.89 at the close of business Tuesday, the rate of change is 0.0125 or 1.25%.

Note that the rate of change is calculated as final value minus initial value all divided by initial value, as shown in Equation 5.1.

$$\text{rate} = \frac{\text{final-initial}}{\text{initial}} = \frac{2,011.89 - 1,987.05}{1,987.05} \approx 0.0125$$
$$(5.1)$$

A 4% rate of return might be made up of a 1.5% per annum rate of time preference, a 2% per annum inflation premium, and a 0.5% interest rate risk premium. In practice, this arithmetic does not always work out. In times of artificially depressed interest rates, the nominal rate of interest might be artificially less than the sum of the rate of time preference, inflation, and the interest rate risk premium. In this case, the nominal rate might not even compensate you for inflation, leaving you worse off in real terms at the end of the term.

Note that there are other components of the interest rate not typically mentioned in an introductory class. For example, you might also need to be compensated for "liquidity risk." For example, long-term investments can be less liquid (i.e., you are less able to turn them back into cash) than short-term investments. You may therefore be less willing to buy less liquid investments, and this reduction in demand should give less liquid investments lower prices, which, other things being equal, translates to a higher expected return to compensate you for the lower liquidity.

Inflation is sometimes of interest in very specific cases. For example, the average price of a house in my city in N.Z. was just under $80,000 25 years ago. This year the average price of a house in my city has been reported as just over $300,000. Essentially the same real good is being described: one average house. The house price inflation rate i per annum in my city therefore roughly satisfies Equation 5.2.

$$\$80,000 \times (1+i)^{25} = \$300,000 \qquad (5.2)$$

Following the dinner party rule (p. 31), dividing both sides of Equation 5.2 by \$80,000, and taking the 25th root, and subtracting 1, yields the following:

$$
\begin{aligned}
\$80,000 \times (1+i)^{25} &= \$300,000 \\
(1+i)^{25} &= \frac{\$300,000}{\$80,000} \\
(1+i) &= \left(\frac{\$300,000}{\$80,000}\right)^{\frac{1}{25}} \\
i &= \left(\frac{\$300,000}{\$80,000}\right)^{\frac{1}{25}} - 1 \\
i &= 3.75^{0.04} - 1 \approx 0.054.
\end{aligned}
$$

That is, average house price inflation in my city has been at the rate of about 5.4% per annum over the last 25 years, well above average N.Z. CPI inflation of only about 2.2% per annum. The 5.4% per annum inflation rate in my city is below average house price inflation in my country as a whole (that number is around 6.5% per annum). So, house prices in my city have advanced more rapidly than the price of a basket of consumer goods, but less rapidly than house prices in the country as a whole.

Suppose house price inflation is exactly 5.4% per annum for the next 25 years (rounding to one decimal place). Can you *inflate* the current average house price in my city to estimate the average house price 25 years from now? Well, we get the estimated average house price 25 years from now as $300,000 \times (1 + i)^{25} = \$300,000 \times (1.054)^{25} \approx \$1,117,214$, that is, roughly 1.1 million dollars.

If we assume house price inflation in my city has been steady at 5.4% per annum for the last 25 years,[3] can you *deflate* today's average house price to estimate the average house price 10 years ago? Well, $\$300,000 \div (1 + i)^{10} = \frac{\$300,000}{(1.054)^{10}} \approx \$177,303$, that is, roughly 177 thousand dollars.

Here is a very common source of confusion among students. Although the actions of inflating and deflating (using house price inflation, or CPI inflation, or some other inflation measure), appear mechanically similar to the actions of compounding and discounting at some market-determined nomi-

---

[3]In practice, of course, house price inflation has not been steady in my city, in N.Z, or in the U.S. over the last 25 years. I am sure you have seen the headlines concerning (and older students or your parents may have been personally affected by) dramatic swings in housing prices.

nal required rate of return, they are not the same things. The difference is that when compounding and discounting, we usually use a nominal interest rate r that includes inflation. That is, we have $r = i+$(other stuff), but when inflating or deflating, we just use the inflation rate i by itself.

CPI index numbers and inflation rates derived from them are useful for adjusting other economic numbers for the general level of consumer prices. The adjusted numbers then allow us to make statements about real purchasing power. For example, I am curious to know whether average salaries have kept pace with inflation or not. So, I could take the time series of average salary figures for the period, say, 1990–2015, and deflate each of them using inflation rates for the period 1990 up to that year to put the salary figures in terms of 1990 dollars.[4] Then I would know whether average salaries have risen or fallen in real terms (measured in 1990 dollars). Only then could I argue whether salaried people are better or worse off in real purchasing power terms

---

[4]Here are some details slightly above the level of the class: Suppose i_t is the CPI inflation rate during year t, for $t = 1990, ..., 2015$, and S_t is the average salary level at the end of year t, then $R_{t,1990} = \frac{S_t}{\prod_{\tau=1990}^{\tau=t}(1+i_\tau)}$ is the average real salary level at the end of year t, measured in beginning-of-year 1990 dollars, where "Π" is the product symbol.

than they were previously.

CPI inflation has a terribly biting impact on investment earnings. If you keep your savings under the mattress, then every dollar you hold decreases in its real purchasing power at the rate of inflation. If you keep your money in some lousy savings account only ever earning less than a percentage point per annum, then your savings will not keep pace with inflation over the long run.

Longer-term bonds usually offer returns that beat inflation. Note, however, that standard bonds offering fixed coupons are nominally denominated. That is, their future cash flows are fixed in advance in nominal terms. So, unexpectedly high inflation can eat into the purchasing power of these fixed future cash flows. Diversified portfolios of stocks are usually inflation beaters over the long run (say, 20+ years), but year-to-year volatility in stock prices means that over the short-term you can easily do worse in stocks than putting your money under the mattress. (See the discussion of risk in Chapter 13.)

Finally, when discounting nominal future cash flows, we always use a nominal interest rate. There are rare occasions, however, where some capital project or other asset is to be valued using forecasts of future cash flows in *real* terms. That is, the forecasts of cash flows do not include the effects of inflation. In these cases, the discount rate should have the inflation rate taken out. That is, nominal cash flows should be discounted using a nominal interest rate, and real cash flows should be discounted using a real interest rate. (Note that neither of these actions correspond to deflating at the inflation rate, as discussed above.) If done correctly/consistently, the asset valuation will be absolutely identical regardless of which approach is used.

Chapter 6

Bonds and Interest Rates

I have some old physical paper bonds. They are financial securities that an investor purchased about 100 years ago. They are printed on nice paper with fine colored engravings, like old bank notes. On the face of each bond is printed the name of the issuer (i.e., the borrower), the date of the issue, the principal (also called the "face value") of the bond, the term to maturity, the coupon rate, and the frequency of the coupon (semi-annual in my case).

Attached to each bond are little paper coupons. Each coupon has a date and an amount on it (they look rather like coupons from your supermarket). The bondholder clipped out a coupon every six months and mailed it to the bond issuer as evidence that they held the bond. Then the company mailed them a check for the coupon amount. It is mostly done electronically nowadays, but the periodic payment on a bond is still called a "coupon," after the old-fashioned paper coupon that the bondholder used to have to clip out and mail in.

First-year finance students usually handle bond problems quite well, but they repeatedly make the same simple mistakes. So, let me address these weaknesses.

When you buy a standard bond, you pay some price for it up front, and then the issuer of the bond promises to pay you a series of coupons, C, and also a final payment of the principal, F (i.e., F for <u>f</u>ace value), as in Figure 6.1.

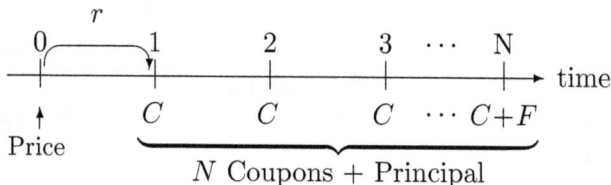

Figure 6.1: Bonds: Cash Flows

What is the price of the bond up front? Well, the price is just the PV of the future cash flows.[1]

In order to be able to price the bond (and this is the most common question asked of students), you need to know the coupons C, the count of coupons N, the principal (or face value) F, and the discount rate r per period.

The easiest of these is the principal. You are usually told by your examiner that the principal is some round dollar amount, like $F = \$1,000$.

I told you to always be on the lookout for annuities. So, I hope it is obvious that the stream of coupons is an annuity. We value that slice of the PV using the annuity formula. ...but what exactly is the amount of the dollar coupon C?

Well, on my old physical paper bonds, the "coupon rate" is printed in black and white alongside the principal amount on the face of the bond,

---

[1]For finance majors (this is above the level of this class): In practice, in the real world, if the bond is purchased *between* coupon dates, then there is an additional calculation for "accrued interest" due the vendor of the bond. A quoted "clean price" ignores the accrued interest, but the buyer pays the "dirty price" (i.e., the clean price plus the accrued interest). For example, if you buy the bond 150 days into a 181-day coupon period, then accrued interest of $150/181 \times C$ is added to the clean price of the bond. Other day-count conventions exist (e.g., assuming 360 days per year).

and it is also printed on every paper coupon. This rate is usually quoted as a percentage (e.g., 6% per annum). For a standard bond, this coupon rate is fixed and unmoving.

Unfortunately, students frequently confuse the fixed coupon rate with the time-varying yield—to be discussed shortly. I think the confusion stems from the fact that the coupon rate and the yield are both percentage rates per annum and they are often numerically close to each other. To reinforce that it is the coupon rate that is fixed, try to picture my old bond. Both the face and the physical paper coupons attached to it have the coupon rate printed upon them in black and white. So, it must be the coupon rate that is fixed. After all, how could the coupon rate ever change if it is printed in black and white on these pieces of paper?

Now, although coupon rates are quoted in annual terms, and students are usually introduced first to bonds that pay coupons only once per year, many real-world bonds pay coupons twice a year (i.e., they pay "semi-annual coupons"). Most students fail, however, to make the connection between the quoting of coupon rates and the quoting of interest rates more generally. So, we need an aside on annual percentage rates (APRs) to get us started.

You Need to Know: APRs and EARs

Most banks quote interest rates to you in annual terms, but they pay your interest more frequently than once per annum. There are dozens of different common day count conventions to figure out the actual cash flows involved in any particular case (Steiner, 2007).

The simplest convention is that the bank quotes an APR, say 6% per annum, with a frequency of payment of m times per year, say $m = 2$ in the case of semi-annual payments. In that case, an interest rate of $r = APR/m = 0.06/2 = 0.03$ would be used for each six-month period. If the cash payments were monthly, we would use $m = 12$. In that case, an APR of "6% per annum with monthly compounding" would correspond to a monthly interest rate of $r = APR/m = 0.06/12 = 0.005$.

A CD at a bank usually earns compound interest. For example, a \$1,000 one-year CD earning 6% per annum with monthly compounding would be worth $\$1,000 \times (1.005)^{12} = \$1,061.68$ (rounding to the penny) at year end. Thus, the compound interest gives an *effective* annual rate (EAR) of about 6.168%.

More generally $EAR = (1 + APR/m)^m - 1$.

Note that the titles APR and EAR are not universal. Be aware that some banks/countries have slightly different names for these concepts.

Now return to our bond pricing discussion. We said that the coupon rate is printed in black and white on the face of the bond and on the coupons; it is fixed. Alongside the coupon rate will also be printed the frequency of payment of the coupons. They might be annual, semi-annual, quarterly, etc.

Suppose our bond offers a coupon rate of 6% per annum with semi-annual coupons. Then this corresponds (via the APR argument just given) to a coupon rate of 3% per six-month period.

Note that in Figure 6.1, I purposely did not say what the length of each time step was. In the case of a semi-annual bond (i.e., a bond paying two coupons per annum), each time step will be six months. In the case of an annual bond (i.e., a bond paying one coupon per annum), each time step will be one year.

Note also that standard bonds always pay coupons "in arrears." That is, if you buy a newly issued bond, the first coupon is one period hence. So, the coupon stream of a newly issued bond always forms an ordinary annuity, and not an annuity due.

Let us assume that our 6% semi-annual bond

has a face value of $F = \$1,000$. Then the dollar coupon per period is given by

$$C = (\text{annual coupon rate})/m \times F,$$

where m is the number of coupons per annum. Continuing with our example, we get

$$C = 0.06/2 \times \$1,000 = \$30,$$

per semi-annual coupon.

How many coupons are there? Well, printed on the face of the bond is the maturity date. For example, our bond might be a 10-year bond. A 10-year bond paying *annual* coupons has $N = 10$ coupons. A 10-year bond paying *semi-annual* coupons has $N = 20$ coupons.

So, in summary, a 10-year 6% semi-annual bond with a face value of $1,000, pays an ordinary annuity of 20 coupon payments, each of $C = \$30$, plus the payment of the $1,000 face value.

To find the price of the bond, we need only discount the coupons as an annuity using our TVM II mathematics, and discount the face value as a lump sum using our TVM I mathematics. ...but what is the discount rate?

Bond market traders evaluate the riskiness of a bond and assign a discount rate to that bond.

This discount rate is called the "yield to maturity" (YTM) or just the "yield." Like coupon rates, and interest rates in general, the yield is typically quoted in annual terms, but with a compounding frequency that matches the coupon frequency. For example, our 10-year 6% $1,000 semi-annual bond might have a yield of 8% per annum. Implicitly, this means that the discount rate is $r = YTM/m = 0.08/2 = 0.04$ per six-month period.

We now have enough information to price our bond: $F = \$1,000$, $C = \$30$, $N = 20$, $r = 0.04$. We use the PV of an ordinary annuity (Equation 4.1) and the PV of a lump sum (second line of Equations 3.6), as shown in Equation 6.1.

$$\text{Price} = \overbrace{\frac{C}{r}\left[1 - \frac{1}{(1+r)^N}\right]}^{PV \text{ of Coupons}} + \overbrace{\frac{F}{(1+r)^N}}^{PV \text{ of Face}} \quad (6.1)$$

$$= \frac{\$30}{0.04}\left[1 - \frac{1}{(1.04)^{20}}\right] + \frac{\$1,000}{(1.04)^{20}}$$

$$= \$407.70979035 + \$456.38694620$$

$$= \$864.09673655,$$

to eight decimal places. (Recall my note about calculator accuracy on p. 61.)

Note that I gave more decimal places than usual for this calculation. One reason is that global bond markets are about 3.5 times the size of global stock markets (Crack, 2017a).[2] Bond market transactions are, therefore, often in quite large size. So, maybe in practice, I will need to multiply my answer by 1,000 or 10,000 or more.

Did you notice that I missed out one step in my safe strategy calculations? I failed to have a guess at what bond price I would get. I did that on purpose, just this one time, because I wanted to point at the bond pricing formula to show you how to make a guess. Let me now give an equilibrium argument (that is, an argument regarding supply and demand and the movement of prices).

In the bond market there are many bonds with fixed maturity dates, fixed face values, and fixed coupons. These bonds exist, however, in an ever-changing marketplace. As the general level of interest rates rises, bonds that offer coupons that are fixed at old-and-low rates become less attractive (because new bonds are being issued on a daily basis and offering coupons in line with the new higher interest rates). So, the prices of the old bonds fall. Another way to say this is that the discount rate on a bond is, in fact, the required rate of return

---

[2]Volatility in stock market prices means, however, that stocks hit the news headlines more frequently than bonds.

on the bond in the market place. The name of this discount rate is the yield to maturity, as mentioned already. So, as market conditions change, and as these required yields move up, say, then we are discounting the fixed cash flows offered by the bonds at ever higher interest rates. Of course, the higher the discount rate, the lower the PV of a future fixed cash flow. So, as yields rise, bonds offering fixed future cash flows fall in price.

From about 1981 to 2015 we went through a period of steadily declining interest rates in the U.S. Sure enough, there were some sub-periods when interest rates were rising, but if you squint and look at the chart, there is a steady downward trend (Crack, 2017a). A long-term trend like this is called a "secular trend" (where "secular" means "for an age"). As interest rates in general fall, and as required yields on bonds in particular fall, bonds offering fixed old-and-high coupons become more attractive, and their prices rise. That is because the lower the discount rate you use to discount a future fixed cash flow, the higher is its PV. Indeed, investors in long-term U.S. Treasury bonds (T-bonds) outperformed investors in the broad U.S. stock market during the 30 years from 1981 to 2011 because the secular decline in interest rates pumped up bond prices (Crack, 2017a).

It can be shown using algebra that if you put into the bond pricing formula a yield that is equal to the coupon rate of the bond, then the bond price you get out of the formula is just the face value of the bond.[3] For example, with our most recent example, if you used a yield of 6% per annum, the price of the 6%-coupon bond would have equaled the face value of the bond (i.e., $1,000 in this case).

Another name for the face value or principal of the bond is the "par value" of the bond. So, when the yield equals the coupon rate (and thus the price equals the face value), the bond is said to be "trading at par" or "a par bond."

I argued previously that as yields rise, bond prices fall, and as yields fall, bond prices rise. So, because it is true that a $1,000 face value bond trades at a price of $1,000 (i.e., it is a par bond) when the yield equals the coupon rate, then it must be true that a $1,000 face value bond will trade at less than par (it is called a "discount bond") if the yield is greater than the coupon rate. Similarly, a $1,000 face value bond will trade at more than par

---

[3]If you are good at algebra, plug $r = C/F$ (i.e., yield equals coupon rate) into Equation 6.1. After cancellation of terms, you should be left only with price $= F$.

(it is called a "premium bond") if the yield is less than the coupon rate.

So, in our most recent example, of the 10-year 6% semi-annual bond with a face value of $1,000, the fact that the yield was 8% per annum means that before I touched my calculator, I knew that the answer for the bond price was going to have to be below $1,000. The market yield of 8% is not terribly far above the fixed coupon rate of 6%, so my guess was that the discount bond would trade not terribly below $1,000; I would have guessed a price of maybe $900. Finding a price of $864 was therefore in the ball park. If I had found a price above $1,000, or well below $1,000, I would have double checked my calculations looking for my error.

I'd like you to now calculate the bond price assuming it is a 10-year 6% *annual* bond with a face value of $1,000 and a yield of 8% per annum. In that case, the coupon is paid $m = 1$ times per annum, and there are $N = 10$ coupons. I get a price of $402.60488394 + $463.19348808 = $865.79837202, to eight decimal places. The price had to be below $1,000 for the same reasons given above (i.e., yield greater than coupon rate). Note also that, other things being equal, annual and semi-annual bond prices are usually very close to each other.

Equilibrium in the Bond Market

Assume I have three equal-risk semi-annual bonds with coupon rates of 6%, 8%, and 10% per annum, each of face value $1,000, each with 10 years to maturity, and each trading at a yield of 8% per annum. Then, the 6% bond's price is $864.10, the 8% bond's price is $1,000, and the 10% bond's price is $1,135.90 (left as an exercise).

These prices reflect the differences in coupons. So, the bonds are fairly priced, and no bond is unattractively priced relative to any other.

Instead of buying the bond, suppose you put the price of one of the bonds (e.g., $864.10 for the 6% bond) into a bank account paying an APR equal to the 8% yield with semi-annual compounding. Then, at the six-month mark you can withdraw a cash flow equal to the first coupon, leaving the remainder invested. At the one-year mark, you can withdraw a cash flow equal to the second coupon, leaving the remainder invested, and so on. At the 10-year mark, the remaining balance will be worth exactly the final coupon plus the face value. This is true for all three of the bonds mentioned. The pricing of each bond at the same yield has leveled the playing field: each bond offers the same rate of return (i.e., the same yield).

Note that debt/bonds are often ranked in terms of the claim paying ability of the borrower. A borrower with extremely strong claim paying ability might get a AAA rating using the Standard and Poor's rating system (the naming varies with rating agency). Ratings from AAA down to BBB− are "investment-grade" debt. A weak firm's debt might get a BB+ or worse rating (also called "non-investment grade," or "speculative grade," or "junk").

One common source of confusion for students is that a single firm is unlikely to have different debt issues carrying a wide range of ratings. Shorter-term obligations or obligations backed by specific assets are likely to have higher ratings, but different bonds from the same firm are unlikely to differ in rating by many notches (AA+ is one notch higher than AA, AA− is one notch higher than BBB+, etc.). Note that a AAA rating signals "prime credit" (the best investment-grade rating), which sits in a category by itself, and, unlike every lower rating down to CCC, there is no AAA- notch just below it.

Countries and territories also have credit ratings on their debt. At the time of writing (i.e., July 2017), the ratings in Table 6.1 held (see p. 90).

Students commonly make two other mistakes concerning credit ratings. First, students cannot remember where the boundary is between investment-grade debt and speculative-grade debt (see Figure 6.1). Second, students confuse the ranking. For example, they think that an A is superior to an AA (perhaps because students are used to an A being the best grade in school).

To address the first mistake, I just remember that BB+ is the highest rated speculative-grade debt (using the Standard and Poor's rating system). It helps that I have seen it stamped on bond offer prospectuses. Perhaps you should use an Internet search engine to find some bond prospectuses for yourself. To address the second mistake, just remember that more "A"s on your grade transcript is better.

Region	Debt Rating	
Australia	AAA	Investment Grade
Canada	AAA	
Switzerland	AAA	
U.S.	AA+	
France	AA	
N.Z.	AA	
U.K.	AA	
Saudi Arabia	A-	
Mexico	BBB+	
Italy	BBB-	
Russia	BB+	Spec. Grade
Pakistan	B	
Venezuela	CCC	
Mozambique	D	

Table 6.1: Country/Territory Debt Ratings

These are a selection of country/territory debt ratings taken from Standard and Poor's in July 2017. They are ordered from best to worst. BBB- and above are investment-grade debt. BB+ and below are speculative-grade (or junk) debt. These ratings are subject to change (e.g., the U.K. rating dropped two notches from AAA to AA a few days after the "Brexit" vote in June 2016).

Chapter 7

Equities and DDMs

Equity is another name for stocks or shares. Equity is a direct ownership stake. In the old days, stocks were sometimes referred to as "internal equity" and bonds were sometimes referred to as "external equity." Nowadays, however, we typically reserve the word "equity" for a direct ownership stake in the assets of the company, rather than a bond-type claim that requires a default before the bondholders can own the assets.

Figure 7.1 shows a "market-value balance sheet" for a company with $1,000 in assets. The assets are financed by, and thus balanced with, $750 of debt and $250 of equity.

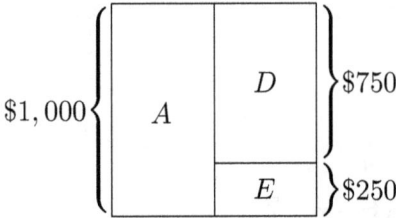

Figure 7.1: Market Value Balance Sheet

The figure shows a market-value balance sheet for a firm with \$1,000 in assets (A). The firm has 75% debt (D) and 25% equity (E).

The equity, or "owners' equity" is the residual claim on the assets of the firm after satisfying the claims of the debtholders. The shareholders can claim the residual cash flows generated by the assets only after these debt claims are paid.

We similarly talk nowadays about having an "equity stake" or "equity" in your own home. Your

------

[1]As an aside, note that the word "mortgage" translates literally from old Middle English or French as "death pledge." It is not that you pledge to pay it off even if you die, but rather that the pledge itself dies when paid off, or when the house is taken over in foreclosure (Crack, 2017a).

equity in your home is the value of your home (i.e., the asset) less the value of your mortgage (i.e., your debt). Other things being equal, your home equity rises when you pay off the mortgage or when real estate prices rise, and falls if you take out a second mortgage or when real estate prices fall.[1]

If real estate prices fall so far that your home's value is less than the value of your mortgage debt, then you have negative equity in your house, and your mortgage is said to be "underwater." Roughly 15 million U.S. homeowners (i.e., one-third of mortgage holders) had underwater mortgages at the peak of the global financial crisis, but this number had dropped to about 8 million by the end of 2014 (Zillow, 2014; Bernstein, 2016), and about 3.2 million by the end of 2015 (BKFS, 2016). Negative equity is also mentioned in the footnote on p. 205.

Stock investing with a long-term horizon is usually recommended for investors seeking to accumulate wealth over their lifetimes. Many financial analysts attempt to value firms that trade on the stock market in order to recommend stocks that investors should buy or sell. At the same time, analysts attempt to value stocks as possible targets for acquisition by firms seeking to expand (because the acquirer needs to know how much to bid). So, valuing a stock is an important challenge.

How then should we value a stock? There are several considerations:

- Fisher (1930, Chapter 1) argues that the worth of any asset is what buyers will pay for it and what sellers will take for it. He says that to assess these, you must have some idea of the future benefits and the rate of interest to translate these future values into present values by discounting.

- Graham and Dodd (1934, p. 325) state that a natural classification of the elements entering into the valuation of common stock would be under three headings: the dividend rate and record; the earning power in the income statement; and, the asset value in the balance sheet.

- Williams (1938, p. 57–58) argues that we need to choose between discounting earnings (i.e., net income) and discounting dividends. He says that when done correctly, either approach will give the same answer (Miller and Modigliani [1961] say the same thing). Williams says that earnings are only a means to an end, and that it is the dividends that are the ultimate end payment to be discounted.

- More generally, how do you value any asset? Damodaran (2012, Chapter 2) argues that there are only three approaches to valuation: DCF, relative valuation (i.e., where you price a similar asset and exploit a common fundamental variable like earnings or sales to price your target asset), and contingent claim valuation (e.g., Black-Scholes option pricing, as in Crack [2017b]).

In this class, we combine the above considerations and we choose a DCF approach to stock valuation, where the cash flows are the dividends of the firm. We assume relatively simple models where the firm pays dividends in some simple pattern. These dividend discount models (DDMs) are simple versions of much more general models (Crack, 2017a; Crack and Roberts, 2018). The more general models even include DDMs for stocks that do not currently pay dividends, but that is beyond this class.

Gordon-Shapiro Growth Model

Let us consider the Gordon-Shapiro growth model (Gordon and Shapiro, 1956). In the simplest version of this model, a dividend of D_0 has just been paid. Dividends grow at constant rate g per period from time $t = 0$ onwards, and the discount rate is r

per period, where $r > g$. Under these assumptions, there are several results as follows:

- The price of the stock at time $t \geq 0$ is given by

$$P_t = \frac{D_t(1+g)}{r-g} = \frac{D_{t+1}}{r-g}. \qquad (7.1)$$

So, in particular,

$$P_0 = \frac{D_0(1+g)}{r-g} = \frac{D_1}{r-g}. \qquad (7.2)$$

- The theoretical price P_t grows at rate g per period. That is because

$$P_t = \frac{D_t(1+g)}{r-g} = \left[\frac{D_t}{r-g}\right](1+g) = P_{t-1}(1+g).$$

- Rearranging $P_t = \frac{D_{t+1}}{r-g}$ to solve for r we get Equation 7.3.

$$r = \frac{D_{t+1}}{P_t} + g \qquad (7.3)$$

That is, the required return on the stock is the sum of the dividend yield and the capital gains rate.[2] Given D_{t+1}, P_t, and g, Equation 7.3 can be used to infer the cost of equity r_E (see p. 144).

---

[2]In practice, most practitioners assume that the dividend yield is the ratio of *trailing* 12-month dividends to price.

- With dividends and price growing at the same rate g, the dividend yield, D_{t+1}/P_t, must be constant. We can deduce $D_{t+1}/P_t = r - g$ from Equation 7.3.

- If $r - g$ is a small number, the theoretical price $P_t = D_{t+1}/(r - g)$ can explode. If $r \leq g$, Equation 7.1 does not apply, because the algebra used to derive Equation 7.1 requires $r > g$.

- Finally, note that if we assume that dividends grow at rate g per period from $t = 1$ instead of from $t = 0$, then we still obtain $P_0 = \frac{D_1}{r-g}$, but it is no longer necessarily true that $D_1 = D_0(1 + g)$. This result will be useful when we get to the multiple-growth rate DDM example in a few pages.

In my experience, Gordon-Shapiro growth model questions are popular, and any plain vanilla scenarios are handled quite well. Students have difficulty, however, with three aspects of the model. First, all but the first of the above six bullet points tend to be a stumbling block for students. (So, I recommend that you study them each carefully.) Second, when the model is rearranged in any way, students get confused. (An example follows in a moment.) Third, students get confused when the

Gordon-Shapiro model is used to model the tail end of a super-normal growth model scenario. (An example follows in the section beginning on p. 100.)

DDM: Gordon-Shapiro Rearranged

Suppose I tell you that $P_0 = \$20$, $D_0 = \$0.50$, and $r = 0.05$ per period, and I want to solve for g. Well, I need to write down an expression that involves the quantities I know, and the unknown g.

I think $P_0 = \frac{D_0(1+g)}{r-g}$ from Equation 7.1 is the obvious place to start. I need to rearrange to solve for g. I will manipulate the formula until I get g on the left-hand side, in Equation 7.4, as follows. (Just be sure to perform the same valid operation to both sides of the equality at each step, as indicated, and then you will still have an equality.)

$$P_0 = \frac{D_0(1+g)}{r-g} \qquad (\times \text{ by } (r-g))$$

$$P_0(r-g) = D_0(1+g) \qquad (\text{expand})$$

$$rP_0 - gP_0 = D_0 + gD_0 \qquad (-D_0 + gP_0)$$

$$rP_0 - D_0 = gD_0 + gP_0 \qquad (\text{collect terms in g})$$

$$rP_0 - D_0 = g(D_0 + P_0) \qquad (\text{swap sides})$$

$$g(D_0 + P_0) = rP_0 - D_0 \qquad (\div \text{ by } (D_0 + P_0))$$

$$g = \frac{rP_0 - D_0}{D_0 + P_0} \qquad (7.4)$$

Now let me have my guess. The value of g will be less than $r = 5\%$ because the Gordon-Shapiro model assumes $g < r$. Economically, g could certainly be negative (because dividends can decrease), but in practice that is unusual in these sorts of problems. So, my first guess is that $0 < g < 5\%$.

Now I can solve my particular problem using Equation 7.4.

$$
\begin{aligned}
g &= \frac{rP_0 - D_0}{D_0 + P_0} \\
&= \frac{(0.05 \times \$20) - \$0.50}{\$0.50 + \$20} \\
&= 0.024390,
\end{aligned}
$$

to six decimal places. I should now plug this answer for g (keeping all the decimal places in my calculator) back into Equation 7.1 to make sure it gives me back $P_0 = \$20$. Yes, it does!

This last example is just one case of rearranging the Gordon-Shapiro model. Another example is to solve for r in terms of the other components, as in Equation 7.3. I will mention this again in Chapter 10 as an "implied DDM" technique to calculate the cost of equity, r_E. You might also be asked to solve for D_0 or D_1 in terms of the other components.

Multiple-Growth Rate DDM

The Gordon-Shapiro model (Equation 7.1), with its assumption of a perpetual constant rate of growth in dollar dividends, is a gross over-simplification of how companies pay dividends in the real world.

A more realistic (though still overly simplified) DDM uses an initial super-normal growth rate in dividends that later settles down to a long-term stable growth rate. The latter part of the problem is modeled using the Gordon-Shapiro constant-growth rate model, and TVM I mathematics is used to combine the initial and latter parts.

My experience has been that the super-normal growth model brings to light most students' inability to apply the Gordon-Shapiro model outside of anything but a plain vanilla scenario. Let us do an example to aid your understanding.

DDM: Super-Normal Growth A company just paid a dividend of $D_0 = \$2.50$ per share. Annual dividends are forecast to grow at a rate of $g_1 = 25\%$ per annum for the next three years. After that, dividends are forecast to grow at rate $g_2 = 6\%$ per annum in perpetuity. The discount rate is $r = 14\%$ per annum. Estimate the current share value.

Do not forget to use as many as possible of the safe strategies I presented previously for solving numerical problems! So, the first thing to do is draw a timeline as in Figure 7.2. It's a little crowded, but it is essential. Having drawn the timeline, now I will

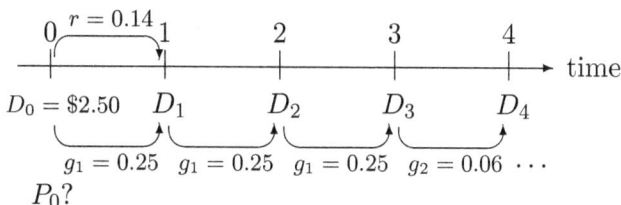

Figure 7.2: DDM: Super-Normal Growth

have a guess. P_0 is just the sum of the discounted dividends $D_1, D_2, \ldots$. I can see that if the growth rate were constant at $g = 6\%$, then the future dividends would be smaller than they are. So, a lower bound on price—using the Gordon-Shapiro model with constant 6% growth rate—is given as follows.

$$
\begin{aligned}
P_0 &= D_0(1+g)/(r-g) \\
&= \$2.50(1.06)/(0.14 - 0.06) \\
&= \$33.125
\end{aligned}
$$

Using $g_1 = 0.25$ for the first three periods instead of a constant 6% will not be enough to double the future dividend stream, so I figure twice this (i.e., \$66.25) should be an upper bound on price. Thus, I expect to find P_0 somewhere between about \$33 and \$66.

The next step is to figure out how to model the dividends on the timeline. You need to walk along the timeline until you come to a point where you can say "Hey, the next dividend grows forever at a constant rate!" In this case, that point is at $t = 2$ (when I can look ahead to the dividend at $t = 3$ that grows from then on at 6% per annum). Then we apply the Gordon-Shapiro growth model at that point (i.e., at $t = 2$) to capture the infinite tail of dividends from $t = 3$ onwards. We then have to discount that $t = 2$ answer back to time zero along with the dividends at times $t = 1$ and $t = 2$.

So, we get that P_0 is given by Equation 7.5.

$$
\begin{aligned}
P_0 &= \frac{D_1}{(1+r)^1} + \frac{D_2}{(1+r)^2} + \frac{P_2}{(1+r)^2} \quad (7.5)\\[2mm]
&= \frac{D_0(1+g_1)}{(1+r)^1} + \frac{D_0(1+g_1)^2}{(1+r)^2} + \frac{D_3}{(r-g_2)}\Big/(1+r)^2\\[2mm]
&= \frac{\$2.50(1.25)}{1.14} + \frac{\$2.50(1.25)^2}{1.14^2} + \frac{D_0(1+g_1)^3}{(0.14-0.06)}\Big/1.14^2\\[2mm]
&= \$2.7412 + \$3.0057 + \frac{\$2.5(1.25)^3}{(0.14-0.06)}\Big/1.14^2\\[2mm]
&= \$2.7412 + \$3.0057 + \$49.9646\\[2mm]
&= \$52.7115,
\end{aligned}
$$

to four decimal places. We can see that this number is right in the middle of my ball-park range. So, there are no red flags.

In my experience, students have two main stumbling blocks in evaluating super-normal DDM problems. First, students do not know where to stop using the TVM I mathematics to discount individual dividends (or, equivalently, where to start using the Gordon-Shapiro model to capture the remaining infinite tail of dividends). The timeline is supposed to help you to implement a simple rule: the last dividend you discount individually is at the point in time where looking ahead one step you can say that that next dividend grows from then on at a perpetual constant rate (i.e., the main assumption of the Gordon-Shapiro model). In our case, I walk along until I get to $t = 2$. Standing at $t = 2$, I can see that, whatever D_3 is, all dividends from then on grow at a constant rate. So, I can apply the $P_t = D_{t+1}/(r - g)$ form of the Gordon-Shapiro model putting D_3 in the numerator[3] and using $g = 0.06$. This gives me the PV at $t = 2$ of

---

[3]Do you ever have difficulty remembering whether the numerator is the top number in a ratio and the denominator is the bottom ratio, or vice versa? Well, "denominator" starts with a "d" and so does "down." Use that trick to remember it.

all dividends after $t = 2$ (i.e., from $t = 3$ onwards). I then have to discount D_1 and D_2 back to zero along with P_2.

Note, as an aside, that I could have stopped discounting individual dividends anywhere from $t = 2$ onwards. For example, I could have discounted the first 10 dividends individually, if I wanted to, and then I would have applied the Gordon-Shapiro model to find P_{10} at $t = 10$ putting D_{11} into the numerator. I would have found the same final answer, after doing a lot more algebra, all of it error prone. The reason I stopped at $t = 2$ is because it is the *first* time I can stop and use the Gordon-Shapiro formula, and thus I minimized the quantity of error-prone calculations I needed to do. If you want to stop later, and discount more dividends individually, then be my guest—but recognize that you are needlessly complicating matters, you are wasting your valuable time, and you are introducing the risk of common errors.

The second main stumbling block for students with supernormal-growth rate DDMs is that they fail to understand what the Gordon-Shapiro model is doing. That is, all it does is capture a perpetual stream of dividends and reduce them to a *PV* at some point in time. In order to use our TVM I mathematics to bring that PV back to $t = 0$ (that is usually the target), we need to know where the PV of the perpetual dividends is located on the timeline. The functional form of the Gordon-Shapiro model (repeating Equation 7.1) is given by

$$P_t = \frac{D_t(1+g)}{r-g} = \frac{D_{t+1}}{r-g}.$$

There are two different formulas hiding in there: $P_t = D_t(1+g)/(r-g)$ and $P_t = D_{t+1}/(r-g)$. I used the second formula because it looks ahead to the next dividend to find P_2. The first formula does not apply at $t = 2$ in our particular example because $D_3 \neq D_2(1+g_2)$. That is because of the change in growth rate in this example. Having obtained a price at $t = 2$, I then need to discount it back two time steps.

Many students get the count of steps needed to discount the tail-end Gordon-Shapiro PV wrong. I suspect it is both because of a failure to draw a timeline, and because they never understood exactly what the Gordon-Shapiro model was doing in the first place. In particular, note that the formula $P_t = D_{t+1}/(r-g)$ gives price at time t (I used $t = 2$) based on a dividend at time $t+1$ (I used D_3). So, if you want to find PV at $t = 0$, you have to discount P_t backwards for t periods ($t = 2$ in this case).

Finally, let me remind you to follow the safe strategies for solving numerical problems. Start with a timeline. Label it properly. Have a guess. Write down the formula you are using in symbolic terms. Then write it out with the numbers. Confirm that your answer is in the ball park, and recompute if not. Plug your answer back into a simpler formula if possible (there might not be a simpler formula in this case).

Chapter 8

Capital Budgeting I: Decision Rules

Capital expenditure (CAPEX; pronounced *cap-ex*) is when firms spend money to invest in a big project. For example, buying a combine harvester is a capital expenditure because the cost of this long-lived asset is capitalized (i.e., recorded as a long-term asset on the balance sheet) and expensed only slowly over time via depreciation as it is "used up." Contrast this with buying, say, a $20 hammer, or paying for heating an office building, both of which are current expenses, even though, realistically, the hammer may outlast the combine harvester.

Firms engaged in capital expenditure typically face a budget constraint (i.e., rationing). "Capital budgeting" is choosing whether to invest or not in any given project and choosing between competing projects; it is capital expenditure on a budget.

The corporate officer responsible for capital budgeting is the chief financial officer (CFO). Decision rules exist to help CFOs decide whether to accept or reject an investment project. The most common rules are the NPV, IRR, and PayBack rules.

Before defining the first two of these rules, let me present results from Graham and Harvey (2001), who asked U.S. CFOs how they make capital budgeting decisions in the real world:

- CFOs "always or almost always" use: the IRR rule (75.6% of respondents), the NPV rule (74.9% of respondents), and the PayBack rule (56.7% of respondents). CFOs use multiple rules simultaneously, so these numbers need not add to 100%.

- Large firms are significantly more likely to use the NPV rule than small firms.

- Small firms are equally likely to use the IRR, NPV, or PayBack rules.

- Decision makers with an MBA degree are more

likely to use the NPV rule. Binder and Chaput (1996) also find this, and that the use of discounting rules is correlated with interest rates (i.e., discounting is more important when interest rates are higher).

- Decision makers without an MBA degree are more likely to use the PayBack rule.

- Some academics hypothesized that the PayBack rule, with its focus on the short-term return of funds, might be attractive to cash constrained firms (i.e., firms that need cash ASAP to avert failure). However, they found no evidence of this.

- Other rules always (or almost always) used include: discounted payback 29.5%; average accounting rate of return 20.3%; and profitability index 11.9%.

Students are very good at executing simple NPV and PayBack rules, but they tend to stumble consistently on a few topics: the IRR rule in general; multiple (or no) IRRs in particular; IRRs for borrowing versus lending projects; mutually exclusive projects with an unlimited budget; and, mutually exclusive projects with a constrained budget.

The NPV Rule

Fisher (1930) presents and explains the "principle of maximum present value." This is what we now call the NPV rule. There is further discussion of Fisher's work in Hirshleifer (1958), Brealey and Myers (1991, p. 22), and in my Chapter 12.

The NPV rule is simply to accept the project or projects that add the most value to the firm (and therefore to shareholder wealth). The value added for any individual project is measured using the NPV formula in Equation 8.1.

$$NPV = \sum_{t=0}^{\infty} \frac{CF_t}{(1+r)^t}, \qquad (8.1)$$

where NPV is the net present value at time $t = 0$, CF_t is the cash flow from the project at time t for $t = 0, 1, \ldots, \infty$, and r is the constant discount rate per period.[1]

We discuss the cash flows CF_t in detail in Chapter 9 and the discount rate r in detail in Chapter 10 and Chapter 11.

We might truncate the summation in Equation 8.1 at $t = T$ for some T using some terminal

---

[1]I could write $NPV_0(r)$ or $NPV(r)$ in Equation 8.1 to indicate that the NPV is a function of the inputs.

value calculation that may involve a perpetuity.

If there is one and only one project to consider, then the NPV rule is to accept the project if $NPV > 0$.[2]

The IRR Rule

Fisher (1930) presents what is essentially our IRR rule (see discussion/clarification in Hirshleifer [1958, p. 346]). The basic IRR rule is that we should set Equation 8.1 equal to zero and solve implicitly for $r = IRR$, as in Equation 8.2, and then accept the project if $IRR > r$, where r is the discount rate.

$$0 = \sum_{t=0}^{\infty} \frac{CF_t}{(1 + IRR)^t},$$
(8.2)

The IRR rule applies only when we have a single project to consider, and that project is a "standard" (or "simple" or "traditional") project (i.e., a project with an initial cash outlay and subsequent cash inflows), and the discount rate is constant.

---

[2]Technically, if $NPV = 0$, then the project's cash flows exactly meet our required rate of return. As such, we should accept the project. In practice, CFOs want $NPV > 0$ by a healthy margin for error. So, I tell my students to assume that $NPV > 0$ is required before a project is accepted.

When we plot $NPV(r)$ versus discount rate r for a standard project, the plot is monotonically downward sloping and passes through $NPV(r) = 0$ at the single point where $r = IRR$. For example, Table 8.1 shows the cash flows to a standard project and Figure 8.1 shows its "NPV profile" with its IRR marked. For discount rates such that $r > IRR$, the $NPV(r)$ is negative, and for discount rates such that $r < IRR$, the $NPV(r)$ is positive. The IRR rule (i.e., accept if $IRR > r$) therefore agrees 100% with the NPV rule for single standard projects.

Timing	Cash Flow
CF_0	$-\$1,000$
CF_1	$+\$600$
CF_2	$+\$500$
CF_3	$+\$400$

Table 8.1: Cash Flows: Standard Project

These cash flows are for a standard project. That is, the project costs money up front, and has subsequent cash inflows. Standard projects have a single IRR. It occurs at 25.3474% (to four decimal places) for this project, as shown in Figure 8.1.

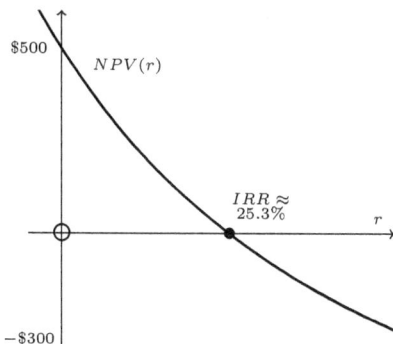

Figure 8.1: $NPV(r)$ versus r: Standard Project

The figure shows the plot of $NPV(r)$ versus discount rate r for the project with cash flows in Table 8.1. There is a single IRR at 25.3474% (to four decimal places). The vertical intercept is at $500 because $NPV(0)$ is just the sum of all the cash flows to the project. The IRR rule agrees 100% with the NPV rule in the case of a standard project, as explained in the text.

If, however, we have competing projects, or projects with non-standard cash flows (i.e., other than a single cash outflow followed by cash inflows), or time-varying discount rates, the IRR rule often fails or cannot even be applied. The next subsection builds upon issues raised in Hirshleifer (1958).

The IRR Rule: Issues

Although the NPV and IRR rules agree for single standard projects, there are many non-standard cases where the IRR rule needs to be considered on a case-by-case basis, or simply does not apply. The following common issues cause confusion.

- It is easy to build a set of non-standard cash flows for which there is a single IRR, but where $NPV(r)$ *increases* with increasing discount rate r. For example, suppose a project has the cash flows in Table 8.2.

Timing	Cash Flow
CF_0	+$100,000
CF_1	−$120,000

Table 8.2: Cash Flows: Borrowing Project

These cash flows are for a borrowing project (as opposed to an investment project). That is, the project generates money up front, which you pay back later. The IRR is 20%, as shown in Figure 8.2.

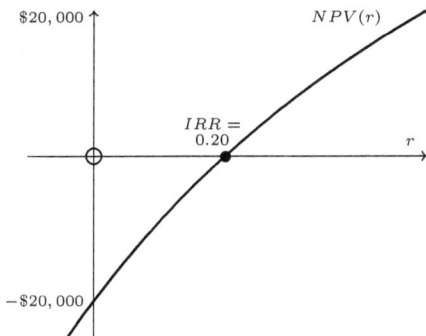

Figure 8.2: $NPV(r)$ versus r: Borrowing Project

The figure shows the plot of $NPV(r)$ versus discount rate r for the project with cash flows in Table 8.2. There is a single IRR at 20%. $NPV(r)$ increases with r because this is a non-standard *borrowing* project. The vertical intercept is at $-\$20,000$ because $NPV(0)$ is just the sum of all the cash flows to the project. If your discount rate is $r < 0.20$ then the NPV is negative (i.e., the borrowing rate of 20% is unattractively higher than what you deem an appropriate borrowing discount rate r). If your discount rate is $r > 0.20$ then the NPV is positive (i.e., the borrowing rate of 20% is attractively lower than what you deem an appropriate borrowing discount rate r). In this simple non-standard case, the IRR rule has to be reversed, but with good economic motivation.

- We can also build a set of non-standard project cash flows for which there are *multiple* IRRs. For example, suppose a project has the cash flows in Table 8.3. Then the plot of $NPV(r)$ cuts the r-axis three times as shown in Figure 8.3, yielding three IRRs.

Timing	Cash Flow
CF_0	$-\$8,000$
CF_1	$+\$39,200$
CF_2	$-\$62,500$
CF_3	$+\$32,200$

Table 8.3: Cash Flows: Multiple IRRs

These cash flows are for a non-standard project with three IRRs (at 15%, 75%, and 100%). See the plot of NPV in Figure 8.3. Advanced students might like to note that the sign changes in the successive cash flows engender sign changes in the successive coefficients of a polynomial in $(1 + r)$ obtained by multiplying Equation 8.1 through by $(1 + r)^3$. Descartes' rule of signs may help you to figure the number of IRRs in cases like this. Please see Osborne (2010; 2014, Chapter 5) for a deep examination of multiple IRR issues.

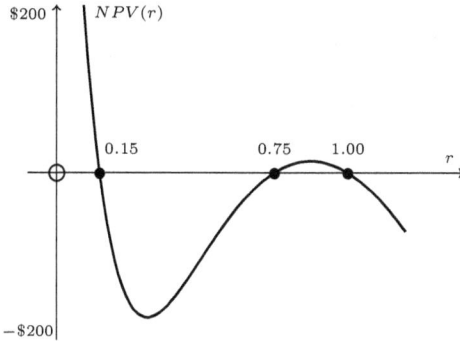

Figure 8.3: $NPV(r)$ versus r: Three IRRs

The figure shows the plot of $NPV(r)$ versus discount rate r for the project with cash flows in Table 8.3. There are three IRRs (at 15%, 75%, and 100%). The vertical intercept (not shown) is at $900 because $NPV(0)$ is just the sum of all the cash flows to the project. Some authors argue that with multiple IRRs, the larger IRRs do not make economic sense and should be ignored. I argue, instead, that this project has investment elements in its cash flow profile (e.g., initial outlay at $t = 0$ and inflow at $t = 1$), and also, overlapping, borrowing elements in its cash flow profile (e.g., cash inflow at $t = 1$ and cash outflow at $t = 2$). So, the project is a hybrid, and no single basic or reversed IRR rule can work. In this case, the simplest rule is the NPV rule: if the NPV is positive, then the project adds value. The IRR rule cannot be used.

- The project with the non-standard cash flows in Table 8.4 has *no* real-valued IRRs. The plot of $NPV(r)$ is positive for every real-valued r, as shown in Figure 8.4. No real-valued IRR exists. If you reverse the sign on every cash flow in Table 8.4, then $NPV(r)$ is negative for every real-valued r. In either case, no real-valued IRR exists, no IRR rule can work, and the NPV rule is required.

Timing	Cash Flow
CF_0	+\$105,000
CF_1	−\$250,000
CF_2	+\$150,000

Table 8.4: Cash Flows: No IRR

These cash flows are for a project with no real-valued IRR. The NPV is positive for all real-valued discount rates. See the plot of NPV in Figure 8.4. No IRR rule can work. Advanced students might like to note that multiplying Equation 8.1 through by $(1 + r)^2$ yields a quadratic in $(1 + r)$. This, in turn, yields complex-valued IRRs of $r = (4 \pm \sqrt{5}i)/21$.

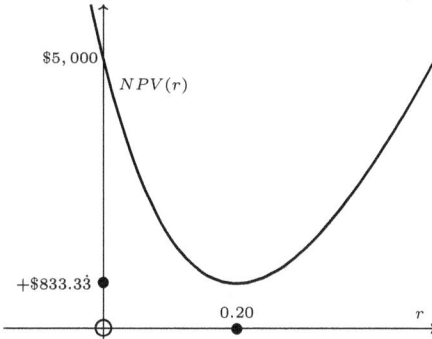

Figure 8.4: $NPV(r)$ versus r: No IRR

The figure shows the plot of $NPV(r)$ versus discount rate r for the project with cash flows in Table 8.4. There are no real-valued IRRs. The vertical intercept is at \$5,000 because $NPV(0)$ is just the sum of all the cash flows to the project. The minimum project value occurs at the point $(r, NPV(r)) = (0.20, \$833.3\dot{3})$. With no real-valued IRR, no IRR rule can work for this project.

- We have just seen examples of non-standard projects where the IRR rule breaks down because there are multiple IRRs or no real-valued IRR (i.e., in these cases, there does not exist a unique IRR to compare with the discount rate). What if the tables are turned and we have a standard project with a single unique IRR, but there are multiple discount rates? That is, we generalize the NPV rule, Equation 8.1, to allow for compounding at time-varying discount rates.

Table 8.5 shows a single standard project with a unique IRR at 12.5%. Two scenarios are given for a known pattern of time-varying future discount rates. In one case, the NPV is positive, and in the other case, the NPV is negative. The IRR, however, is driven by project cash flows alone, and is thus blind to varying discount rates.

Could the answer be to compare the IRR with the geometric average discount rate $\bar{r}_{geom}$? No, this does not work because $\bar{r}_{geom}$ is the same for both scenarios, even though the NPVs are of different signs. (The arithmetic average discount rate is also the same in both scenarios.) Thus, the IRR rule fails again, but in this case it is because there is no unique discount rate to compare the IRR with.

Timing (t)	Cash Flow	$r_A(t)$	$r_B(t)$
CF_0	$-\$75,000$	—	—
CF_1	$+\$30,000$	0.10	0.15
CF_2	$+\$61,172$	0.15	0.10
NPV	—	$+\$630$	$-\$556$

Table 8.5: IRR and Time-Varying Discount Rates

These cash flows are for a standard project with a unique IRR at 12.500% (to three decimal places). The discount rate $r_A(t)$ or $r_B(t)$ is for the period ending at time t. Under Scenario A (B), discount rates rise (fall) over time. Note how the discounting works (i.e., generalizing Equation 8.1 to allow for compounding at time-varying discount rates):

$$NPV_A = -\$75,000 + \frac{\$30,000}{(1.10)} + \frac{\$61,172}{(1.10) \times (1.15)},$$

and

$$NPV_B = -\$75,000 + \frac{\$30,000}{(1.15)} + \frac{\$61,172}{(1.15) \times (1.10)}.$$

The geometric average discount rate is given by $\bar{r}_{geom} = [(1.10) \times (1.15)]^{1/2} - 1 = 12.472\%$, to three decimal places, in both scenarios. The arithmetic average discount rate is $\bar{r}_{arith} = 12.500\%$ in both scenarios. NPVs are rounded to the dollar.

- Finally, it is tempting to think of a standard project's IRR as a "rate of return" on the project, akin to the rate of return on a bank account where you keep your money invested. Unlike your bank account, however, intermediate project cash flows that get thrown off and not reinvested back into the project are not *reinvested* at the IRR.[3] (Note that the IRR rule assumes that intermediate *negative* cash flows are *financed* at the IRR.) So, the IRR may overstate the rate of return on a project. The yield to maturity on a bond has the same problematic reinvestment interpretation.

Competing Projects

Here is a classic question guaranteed to trip over half the students in the class.

Question: Suppose you have two mutually exclusive standard projects A and B (i.e., each has an initial outlay at $t = 0$ and inflows after that). Sup-

---

[3]For finance majors, given that positive (negative) cash flows are not reinvested (financed) at the IRR, Hirshleifer (1958, p. 351) makes the point that the *internal* rate of return is not really *internal*.

pose that project A has an initial outlay of $150,000 and $NPV_A = +\$1,000,000$ and project B has an initial outlay of $175,000 and $NPV_B = +\$750,000$. Suppose that your firm has an unlimited capital budget (i.e., it has enough financing on hand to take on any and all projects that add to shareholder wealth). What should you do? Please choose one of the following options:

(a) Accept project A only.

(b) Accept project B only.

(c) Accept both project A and project B.

(d) Accept neither project A nor project B.

My experience has been that half my students will choose answer (c). They think that the unlimited capital budget means that they can and should take on both positive-NPV projects.

In fact, the correct answer is (a), because the projects are described as *mutually exclusive*. That is, you can take one or the other, but not both. For example, should I turn a vacant warehouse beside the campus into noisy student apartments or a quiet study center? I cannot have both projects because they conflict. Taking one project *excludes* the possibility of taking the other project. When considered together, they are *mutually exclusive.*

The following are often confusing points regarding competing projects.

- "Mutually exclusive" means you cannot take more than one of the projects. When you see the words "mutually exclusive," a mental light bulb should flash immediately to remind you that you will choose either one of them, or none of them, but you cannot have both of them.

- The IRR and NPV rules may at first appear to conflict for competing projects of different scale. (Small-scale high-IRR projects may add much less value than large-scale low-IRR projects.)

  For example, suppose there are two mutually exclusive projects A and B with cash flows as shown in Table 8.6. At any sensible discount rate (e.g., $r = 0.10$, as shown in the table), both projects have positive NPVs. Although Project A has an IRR twice that of Project B, Project B adds much more value. If you misunderstood the IRR rule, then you may at first think that the IRR and NPV rules have a ranking conflict here.

  In fact, let me remind you that the IRR rule does not say that you should take the project with the

Timing	Project A Cash Flows	Project B Cash Flows
CF_0	−$100	−$10,000
CF_1	+$200	+$15,000
$NPV(r = 0.10)$	$82	$3,636
IRR	100%	50%

Table 8.6: Projects of Different Scale

These cash flows are for small-scale Project A (with a very high IRR) and large-scale Project B (with a smaller IRR). The NPV is shown at $r = 0.10$, rounded to the nearest dollar. The two projects are mutually exclusive.

highest IRR. It says, rather, that for a single standard project, if the discount rate $r < IRR$, then the project adds value. In this case, both the IRR and NPV rules tell you that for any reasonable discount rate, the projects in Table 8.6 both add value. There is no conflict between the rules because the IRR rule does not take account of scale, and so it does not say anything about the size of the value added. Given the competition between the two projects, we have to use the NPV rule in this case. Nevertheless, any investor would rather spend their \$10,000 on 100 copies of project *A* (if that were even possible) than on project *B*, and you have to use both the IRR and NPV rules in concert in this case to deduce this.

We might also conclude that the NPV rule is biased away from smaller projects, because smaller-scale projects tend to have lower NPVs.

- The IRR and NPV rules may also appear to conflict for projects with different cash flow timing.

  For example, suppose mutually exclusive Projects *C* and *D* have cash flows as shown in Table 8.7. At low-to-medium sensible discount rates (below $r = 11.35\%$ in this case), the NPV of project *D* is larger than the NPV of project *C* (i.e., the opposite ranking of the IRRs), and we prefer Project *D*, even though Project *C* has the higher IRR. For example, NPVs at $r = 0.10$ are shown in the table.

  Project *C*'s IRR is high because its large early cash flow (relative to Project *D*) pushes up its IRR—a useful signal from the IRR calculation. Again, if you misunderstood the IRR rule, then you may at first think that the IRR and NPV rules have a ranking conflict here.

Timing	Project C Cash Flows	Project D Cash Flows
CF_0	$-\$10,000$	$-\$10,000$
CF_1	$+\$12,500$	$\$0$
CF_2	$\$0$	$\$0$
CF_3	$\$0$	$+\$15,500$
$NPV(r = 0.10)$	$\$1,364$	$\$1,645$
IRR	25.00%	15.73%

Table 8.7: Projects with Different Payout Profiles

These cash flows are for Project C and Project D with different cash flow profiles. The NPV is shown at $r = 0.10$, rounded to the nearest dollar. The two projects are mutually exclusive.

Let me remind you, however, that the IRR rule does not say that you should take the project with the highest IRR. It says that for a single standard project, if the discount rate $r < IRR$, then the project adds value. Both projects in Table 8.7 add value for discount rates below their respective IRRs. Again, the NPV rule tells us which one adds the most value, and the IRR rule cannot be used to choose which project to take.

- Given limited capital, and a menu of projects to choose from, some of which are mutually exclusive, we need to determine which feasible combination of projects on the menu has the best combined NPV. Given the complexity, we may need an optimization routine to solve this problem.

- The bottom line is that there is no circumstance under which we can reliably use the IRR rule to choose between competing projects. The IRR rule does give us a measure of bang-for-our-buck that is missing from the NPV rule, but the IRR rule does not tell us which project(s) add(s) most value.

Finally, let me remind you again to follow the safe strategies for solving these numerical problems. It really makes a difference. Start with a timeline. Label it properly. Have a guess. Be on the lookout for annuities. Write down the formula you are using in symbolic terms. Then write it out with the numbers. Confirm that your answer is in the ball park, and re-compute if not. Plug your answer back into a simpler formula if possible (there might not be a simpler formula in this case).

Chapter 9

Capital Budgeting II: Cash Flows

Accountants use financial statements to create a dozen different common measures of flow. There are top-line revenues, bottom-line earnings after taxes, cash flows, EBIT, EBITDA, and adjusted values of each of these (Graham, 2006, Chapter 12). Which cash flow measure should we put into the numerator of an NPV calculation for capital budgeting?

Answering this question is the deepest conceptual part of the class. Students, however, tend to handle this fairly well in exams, because they just follow mechanical rules to implement the cash flow estimation. I will focus only on the conceptual part, which should be of interest to anyone wanting to gain a better understanding.

The cash flows we want to discount are the unlevered FCFs to suppliers of capital. Let me explain some of these words before going into deeper detail.

- We focus on the project as if it is a mini-firm. So, we can think about a balance sheet for the project with assets on the LHS, and financing in prudent proportions (see Chapter 10) on the RHS.

- The word "unlevered," in this context, means without regard to financing. (See also the box on "leverage" on p. 133.) That is, we want to value the *assets* of the project by discounting the cash flows generated by them, without regard to how the assets are financed. So, for the FCF, the focus is on the LHS (i.e., asset side) of the balance sheet, without regard to the RHS (i.e., financing side) of the balance sheet. (See, however, the final note on financial distress starting on p. 205.)

- The phrase "free cash flow" (FCF) refers to cash flow that can float freely away from the business operations. That is, cash flow that is free and clear of the operating needs of the project. For example, it could be residual cash flow after you pay for salaries, lighting, heating, council taxes, re-stocking inventory, accounting for the benefit of the tax deductibility of depreciation, any necessary CAPEX, payment of taxes, etc. If a firm generates positive FCF, it can use the money to pay interest on the debt, pay principal on the debt, pay dividends, or even repurchase stock (see Chapter 16).

- The phrase "to suppliers of capital" means cash flows available to the suppliers of equity and debt capital. So, for example, we do not deduct interest when calculating FCF available to suppliers of capital because interest is not a cash outflow that reduces cash available to suppliers of capital. Rather, interest *is* a cash flow to suppliers of capital and thus has no net effect on FCF available to capital. This goes hand-in-hand with the "unlevered" perspective. That is, we want to calculate FCF generated by the *assets* of the project (i.e., over and above that consumed by the operations of the project) and we want to add up the cash flows available to be paid out to debtholders and shareholders, without regard to the RHS of the balance sheet.

- Further to this, interest payments on debt are tax

deductible. This tax deduction is beneficial to the firm because it lowers the cost of debt. This tax benefit is not, however, part of the unlevered FCF to capital calculation. Rather, we shall account for this tax benefit in the discount rate (see Chapter 10). If this tax benefit were also in the FCF, then we would be double counting it.

Understanding the exclusion of financing costs from the FCF calculation has always been a stumbling block for students. To help you further, there are two "thinking questions" following.

Question #1: Suppose a debtholder is worried about whether the assets of a firm will generate enough cash flow to pay the interest on the debt this year. The debtholder asks "how much cash is being generated that is free to cover the interest payments?" The debtholder may want to calculate the FCFs generated by the assets of the firm and available to the suppliers of capital. In this calculation, should the interest payments to the debtholder be subtracted as part of the FCF calculation?

Answer #1: No, because subtracting these payments defeats the purpose of calculating FCF available to make the payments in the first place.

You Need to Know: Leverage

In physics, leverage magnifies the force you can exert, usually via a lever resting on a fulcrum.

In finance, "financial leverage" means the use of debt financing. Financial leverage is also called "gearing" (obviously a physics reference to gears).

Financial leverage increases volatility in corporate cash flows and increases beta. It also magnifies gains or losses to investments in a brokerage account (via a margin loan), etc. P/E ratios are also sensitive to leverage, but the direction depends upon the particular circumstances (Crack, 2017a).

We also talk about "operating leverage" in finance. Operating leverage is fixed costs dividend by total costs. In a firm with high operating leverage, bottom line earnings numbers (e.g., EBIT) are very sensitive to changes in revenues.

So, *financial* leverage magnifies the return we can earn on our equity stake (using debt as the fulcrum), and *operating* leverage magnifies the return we can earn on the fixed assets (using fixed costs as the fulcrum).

Question #2: Suppose you start a sole proprietorship with personal funds and you are the sole supplier of capital to the business. Suppose you set up a spreadsheet to forecast before-tax FCFs generated by the business so that you can figure out what cash flow will be available to you each year as compensation for being the sole supplier of capital (and reported as pre-tax income on your personal tax forms). As a part of forecasting what cash flow is going to be available for you to extract, would you deduct projected salary payments to yourself as an operating expense and look only at what is left over as being available as compensation?

Answer #2: No, this makes no sense for a sole proprietorship, where all income is personal income and separating out your salary (for human capital) from the financing costs (for financial capital) is an artificial distinction. You cannot lend money to yourself. Note, however, that if you launch a start-up company and you lend money to the company (a legal person in its own right), and you also pay yourself a salary, then you do deduct your salary from the FCF calculation as an operating expense in order to figure out how much is left over as a return on the invested capital. Outside of the accounting/tax statements for the company, your salary is personal income on your personal tax forms, and the interest payments on the debt are investment income on your personal tax forms. (Unlike the case of the sole proprietorship, your interaction with the company is an "arm's length" transaction.)

Incremental After-Tax Cash Flows

The FCFs are incremental after-tax cash flows. When looking at incremental after-tax cash flows, we ask "What will change if we adopt the project?" That is, what is the incremental effect of taking on the project? For example, are there extra costs up front in the form of CAPEX or a run up in net working capital (NWC)? What are the operational cash flows each period? Does the project cannibalize existing operational cash flows (e.g., when liquid-crystal displays cannibalized cathode ray tube displays)? Does a run up in NWC unwind at project termination? Is there some salvage-value-related tax effect?

Watch out for "opportunity costs." For example, if you build a supermarket on a piece of land you already own, the land is not free. If your next best alternative was going to be to sell the land and have that cash inflow, then by building you lose the opportunity to get that cash inflow. So, you must charge this opportunity cost as a startup cost.

We must also be aware of "sunk costs" (i.e., irreversible old costs). These are not affected by the accept/reject decision and should be ignored. For example, the *original cost* of the land just mentioned is a sunk cost; it does not change in any way whether we take the project on or not. The *current market value* of the land is, however, an opportunity cost if we lose the opportunity to sell the land by taking on the project.

FCF Components

FCF has four main components:

- +Operating Cash Flow (+OCF)

- −Changes in Net Working Capital (−ΔNWC)

- −CAPEX

- +Sundry tax effects (Note: These are not the tax shield from depreciation or interest on debt.[1])

Let us walk through these components one at time.

---

[1]These are called "tax shields" because the tax-deductibility of depreciation and interest expenses reduces revenues, thus shielding you from some taxes.

FCF Component: +OCF

I usually write operating cash flows as

$$OCF = (REV - VC - FC) \times (1 - T) + (DEPN \times T),$$

where REV is revenues, VC is variable costs, FC is fixed costs, T is the tax rate, and $DEPN$ is depreciation. This is the "depreciation tax shield" approach to OCF. Note that the non-cash depreciation expense is not subtracted from revenues, but that the cash tax shield from depreciation is appended. Financing costs, like interest, do not appear here (remember that OCF is generated by the assets on the LHS of the balance sheet).

A mathematically equivalent "pro forma" approach to OCF is a common alternative. In this case, with $OP.EXP$ standing for operating expenses,

$$
\begin{aligned}
OCF &= EBIAT + DEPN \\
&= EBIT \times (1 - T) + DEPN \\
&= \left(REV - \underbrace{OP.EXP}_{\text{incl. } DEPN} \right) \times (1 - T) + DEPN \\
&= [REV - (VC + FC + DEPN)] \times (1 - T) \\
&\qquad\qquad\qquad\qquad\qquad\qquad + DEPN,
\end{aligned}
$$

where, in practice, my first line above should really be $OCF = EBIAT + DEPN + ONCA$, where

$ONCA$ is other non-cash adjustments, like amortization of goodwill, patents, and other intangibles.

Some texts use "Net Income" (NI) to refer to $EBIAT = EBIT \times (1 - T)$. Although technically correct (it is $EBIT$ net of taxes), this is a little confusing. I would rather think as follows:

$$EBIAT = \left(REV - \underbrace{OP.EXP}_{\text{incl. } DEPN} \right) \times (1 - T)$$

$$NI = \left(REV - \underbrace{OP.EXP}_{\text{incl. } DEPN} - INT \right) \times (1 - T),$$

where INT is interest costs on debt. From an unlevered perspective (i.e., no debt) $EBIAT$ and NI would be the same, but more generally they need not be so.

Finally, let me repeat that OCF should not include interest because interest is a *financing* cost not an *operating* cost, and the "O" in OCF stands for operating. That is, OCF is generated by the assets on the LHS of the balance sheet.

FCF Component: $-\Delta$NWC

Net working capital is the difference between current assets (CA) and current liabilities (CL):

$$NWC = CA - CL.$$

Many projects require a run up in NWC at their launch (e.g., stocking the shelves of a new supermarket). This investment into NWC is analogous to a loan. That is, the firm supplies capital to increase NWC at the beginning of the project, and recovers that capital at the end of the project. The supply of NWC at the launch is a drain on the firm's resources and has a negative impact on FCF. (A deeper note on NWC appears in a box on p. 142.)

FCF Component: −CAPEX

Capital Expenditure (CAPEX) is defined as follows:

$$
\begin{aligned}
CAPEX \ = \ & Net\ PPE\ \text{(current)} \\
& - \ Net\ PPE\ \text{(prior)} \\
& + \ DEPN,
\end{aligned}
$$

where PPE is the book value of property, plant and equipment.

"Net" PPE means that the book value is the original cost less accumulated depreciation. In practice, CAPEX is the easiest component for us. It is usually a big outlay at $t = 0$, and nothing else. It may include such items as installation costs or shipping costs for a big machine. In simple examples, CAPEX is typically zero during operational years because the difference between Net PPE (current) and Net PPE (prior) is just $-DEPN$, so $CAPEX = 0$.

We should include here any tax effect in the terminal salvage value of the PPE. That is, if salvage value is different from book value, then there is a tax effect, because you are selling the PPE for a price different from the recorded book value. Note that book value = initial cost $-$ accumulated depreciation, so the after-tax salvage (ATS) value is

$$ATS = \text{salvage} - \underbrace{T \times \overbrace{(\text{salvage - book value})}^{\text{taxable profit or loss}}}_{\text{tax on taxable profit (or tax credit)}},$$

where "salvage" is the selling price of your PPE.

As mentioned in Chapter 8, ultimately, big-ticket PPE purchases get pushed through the income statement as expenses as they get "used up." This is an accounting-motivated technique to match income with expenses as you walk through time.[2] In other words, big-ticket PPE purchases are initially capitalized (that is, recorded as a long-term

---

[2]Note, however, that freehold land is not usually depreciated. By the same token, a perpetual right (e.g., the government-granted right to import rice into Malaysia) is not amortized. In both cases, this is because the asset, tangible or intangible, is infinitely lived, and is thus not being used up.

asset on the balance sheet), but a slice of the original CAPEX for the PPE appears as a depreciation expense (i.e., a book entry) in the income statement each year. The accumulated depreciation is then offset against original PPE to appear as Net PPE (i.e., net book value) each year. If you sell the PPE for more than the reported net book value, then you pay tax on the gain.

FCF Component: +Sundry Tax Effects

This includes items such as changes in deferred taxes. It is often omitted from introductory finance classes.

Job Interview Question: You and I are to play a game. You roll a die until a number other than a one appears. When such a number appears for the first time, I pay you the same number of dollars as there are dots on the upturned face of the die, and the game ends. What is the expected payoff to this game?

Taken from *Heard on The Street: Quantitative Questions from Wall Street Job Interviews*,
©2017 Timothy Falcon Crack. See advertisements at the end of this book.

Deeper Note on NWC

In a higher-level finance class, we would note that although cash is usually part of CA, and although CA appears as part of NWC, our FCF measure uses NWC *excluding* cash on the balance sheet. Cash on the balance sheet has no place in our calculations of FCF because we are solving for cash needs. Cash is, in effect, the "plug figure," so we leave it out of everything else.

Also, the OCF items REV and OP.EXP may include non-cash items in the form of changes to accounts receivable (A/R) and accounts payable (A/P). In that case, the ΔNWC will also include changes in A/R and A/P (and inventory) and will account for the discrepancy.

Finally, note that increases in inventory or A/R need to be financed, whereas decreases in A/P reduce the financing needs. These impacts on FCF are felt through ΔNWC.

At an introductory level, we typically just assume cash sales and cash costs to simplify. We also typically assume a single run up in NWC at launch, level NWC during the project, and a single run down in NWC at termination.

Chapter 10

Capital Budgeting III: Cost of Capital

Valuation requires that we discount cash flows at a rate of return that reflects the level of interest rates and the riskiness of the cash flows (Williams, 1938; Burrell, 1960). In the CAPM chapter (Chapter 12), we will argue that we also need to know the market risk premium. Collectively, these determine the discount rate.

I argue in Chapter 11 that although the objective of the business is to maximize *shareholder* wealth, we should discount FCF using a discount rate that accounts for *all* sources of capital—

typically both shares/equity and debt.

The discount rate is the "weighted average cost of capital" (WACC), as shown in Equation 10.1.

$$r_{WACC} = (w_E \cdot r_E) + [w_D \cdot r_D \cdot (1 - T)], \quad (10.1)$$

where r_E is the cost of equity capital, r_D is the cost of debt capital, w_E is the weight of equity in the WACC, $w_D = 1 - w_E$ is the weight of debt in the WACC, and T is the corporate tax rate.

Let us walk through each component of the WACC. Most of my discussion follows Crack (1996).

- **The Cost of Equity r_E:** Graham and Harvey (2001) say that one in three CFOs always or often use the single-factor CAPM to calculate the cost of equity component of the WACC in capital budgeting. Another one-third always or often use a multi-beta CAPM with additional risk factors in this order of popularity: interest rates, FX, GDP/business cycle, unexpected inflation, size, commodity price risks, term structure risks, financial distress, book-to-market, and momentum (Graham and Harvey, 2001). So, in total, two-thirds of CFOs always or often use a CAPM-type model for capital budgeting. Another 40% always or often use historical average stock returns, and another 16% always or often infer the cost of equity from a DDM (e.g., plug in actual stock price, dividends, and growth rate in dividends, and deduce the discount rate using Equation 7.3 on p. 96).

In this class, the focus is usually on using the CAPM (Chapter 12) to estimate r_E, though many instructors also teach the implied DDM approach. On the CAPM front, estimation of the risk-free rate R_F and the market risk premium $[E(R_M) - R_F]$ are discussed in Chapter 12. So, let us focus only on the CAPM beta here.

In practice, in a first undergraduate finance class, the instructor will probably just give you the equity beta to use. In a first MBA finance class, however, you will likely have to calculate the equity beta via a "comparables" method.

To calculate the equity beta, find companies in a comparable line of business to the project (or acquisition target) under consideration and measure the equity betas of those firms using OLS regressions of their stock returns on returns to a market index (or using published equity betas). Let $\beta_{EQ}^{(COMP)}$ be the equity beta from a comparable firm. I told you that leverage increases betas. So, we need to unlever the equity beta from the comparable company using the market value of the debt and equity of the comparable firm. This yields an asset beta as shown in Equation 10.2.

$$\beta_A^{(COMP)} = \left[\frac{MV\left(EQ^{(COMP)}\right)}{MV\left(EQ^{(COMP)}\right) + MV\left(D^{(COMP)}\right)} \right] \cdot \beta_{EQ}^{(COMP)} \tag{10.2}$$

Which debt do we use? When levering or unlevering betas, we use all forms of long-term debt that pay interest and which are (or will be) part of the permanent capital structure of the firm.

You should get asset betas from several comparable firms, and use the average $\bar{\beta}_A^{(COMP)}$. Having obtained the asset beta, we now need to re-lever it for our own financing to yield an equity beta to feed into the CAPM, as shown in Equation 10.3.

$$\beta_E = \bar{\beta}_A^{(COMP)} \cdot \left(\frac{D + E - EC}{E} \right), \tag{10.3}$$

where D is debt, E is equity, and EC is excess cash. Note that including excess cash in Equation 10.3 makes my presentation a little more general than just the case of a CFO considering an

investment project. That is, if a company is looking at acquiring the assets of a target firm, the
excess cash in that case may be on the balance
sheet of the acquirer, but it is not part of the
permanent capital structure of the acquirer.

Note also that we unlever using market values
(Equation 10.2), but we re-lever using book values (Equation 10.3). Further discussion of the
weights appears after discussion of the cost of
debt.

- **The Cost of Debt r_D**: The cost of debt should
  be a project-specific cost for this project. It need
  not be the cost of debt of the acquirer (without
  loss of generality let me call the firm considering
  the investment the "acquirer"). Indeed, if the
  acquirer is diversified, using its cost of debt could
  effectively subsidize the project.

  The cost of debt could come from the yield on
  the debt of comparable firms. It could come from
  project-specific project financing offers.

- **The Weights of Equity and Debt w_E, and
  w_D**: The weights of equity and debt appearing
  in the WACC are also used (if needed) for re-
  levering the asset beta from the comparables in

Equation 10.3. Let me make several points about these weights as follows.

○ In an undergraduate first class in finance, the instructor will likely just give you the weights.

○ The weights are those that in the eyes of the acquirer represent the riskiness inherent in the FCF generated by the assets of the project (or target company).

○ The weights represent prudent leverage for an investment in this line of business.

○ The weights are judgmental.

○ The weights certainly need not be the weights of the acquirer, nor need they be the "acquisition weights" (i.e., the weights in the acquirer after raising capital for the acquisition).

○ The weights can come from industry averages, as opposed to the weights used in the funding of the particular project.

○ Because the valuation is from the point of view of the acquirer, if the acquirer explicitly states what it views as prudent leverage for this project, then these weights should be used regardless of industry averages, and especially so if these are the weights in the acquiring company and it is in the same line of business as the project.

- **The Corporate Tax Rate T**: When figuring which cash flows to use in Chapter 9, we ignored the interest costs on debt. We argued that these payments do not reduce FCF available to suppliers of capital, because they *are* cash flows to suppliers of capital.

  Interest on debt is, however, tax deductible. We account for this tax shield benefit by reducing the cost of debt by the multiplicative factor $(1 - T)$ in Equation 10.1, where T is the corporate tax rate. That is, we put the after-tax cost of debt $r_D \cdot (1 - T)$ into the WACC in Equation 10.1.

- **The WACC r_{WACC}**: If you had to calculate an equity beta by unlevering/re-levering betas from comparables, you may have noticed that the WACC is relatively insensitive to the weights. For example, if the acquirer uses a high leverage ratio, then the re-levered equity betas will be large, but, offsetting this, the weight of equity in the WACC will be small. These counterbalancing effects should tend to cancel out to some extent (I am not suggesting they offset perfectly).

Chapter 11

Capital Budgeting IV: A Paradox

There is an issue regarding maximization of shareholder wealth that I have never seen explained by anyone. This short topic is over and above the class, so you can skip this chapter if you wish, but it is here for completeness.

The CFO is supposed to seek out positive NPV investments, where NPV is the incremental change in present value of the assets of the firm attributed to a project, and calculated by discounting future FCFs generated by the assets of the project at a rate of return that accounts for the costs of all providers of capital (i.e., both equity and debt).

If, however, our goal is *shareholder* wealth maximization, then why do we conduct capital budgeting by discounting FCFs to the *assets* of the corporation at the required return to *all* providers of capital (i.e., the WACC)? Why not just discount incremental cash flows to *equity* holders at the required return to *equity* (i.e., r_E)? It seems counterintuitive to do otherwise—if the stated objective is correct.

As mentioned previously, Brealey and Myers argue that the NPV rule dates back to Fisher (1930) (Brealey and Myers, 1991, p. 22). (I discuss Fisher in much more detail in Chapter 12.) In explaining the rule, however, neither Fisher nor Brealey and Myers address my concern.

Let me resolve the paradox. Suppose that a new project will have an initial outlay I_0. Suppose that the project will be funded by issuing debt and equity of D_0 and E_0, respectively, in prudent proportions so that $I_0 = D_0 + E_0$.

Assume that the new project requires assets of value A but at cost I_0. (Value is expected to differ from cost here because the firm adds value via new products or processes protected by a first-mover advantage or by patents, etc.) Then A is simply the PV of the FCFs generated by the new assets: $A = \sum_t \frac{FCF_t}{\left(1+r_{WACC}\right)^t}$.[1]

If we assume that the debt is to be repaid out of the FCFs, then $D_0 = \sum_t \frac{BondPayment_t}{(1+r)^t}$, where r is the yield on the debt per coupon period.[2]

The residual cash flow $Residual_t = FCF_t - NetBorrowing_t - BondPayment_t$ then accrues to the shareholders, and adds value $E = \sum_t \frac{Residual_t}{(1+r_E)^t}$ to the equity side of the balance sheet. (Note that $NetBorrowing_t$ is principal paid less principal raised, and the $Residual_t$ cash flows are called "FCF to equity" or "levered FCF," that is, FCFs *after* debt-related cash flows are subtracted.)

Note that E_0 likely does not equal E. For example, perhaps $E_0 = \$1,000,000$ of equity was raised to invest in a project that created $E = \$1,200,000$ worth of value for shareholders.

It must be true that the value of the new assets equals the value of the debt plus the value of the

---

[1]This assumes that there is no excess cash sitting in the balance sheet. See the related discussion of enterprise value in Crack (2017a).

[2]Note that if the new project impacts the existing assets, equity, or debt, or changes the cost of equity r_E or cost of debt r_D, then any such impact should be included in the free cash flows FCF_t.

equity: $A = D_0 + E$. The NPV of the new project is $NPV = A - I_0$. Substituting in for A and I_0 yields $NPV = A - I_0 = (D_0 + E) - (D_0 + E_0) = E - E_0$. That is, in theory, calculating NPV by discounting unlevered FCFs at the WACC gives the *same* answer as discounting levered FCFs at the cost of equity (treating E_0 as a cash outflow from shareholders). In other words, there is no paradox.

So, given that the answers are the same, why choose to discount unlevered FCFs at the WACC? Perhaps the choice stems from firm-level DCF analysis, where an unstable capital structure can confound valuation (e.g., temporarily negative levered FCFs, if debt is being paid down, are misleading). Unstable capital structure is not an issue for NPV analysis, however, because incremental cash flows and prudent capital structure weights are supposed to be used. So, perhaps it is just firm-level DCF habit carried over to project-level NPV analysis.

The bottom line is that SWM is, by definition, about the creation of firm value accruing to shareholders as the *residual* claimants on the firm's assets, after the debtholders' claims. So, the only way to get a positive NPV is if the new project generates FCFs that are sufficient to *both* service the debt and leave residual cash flow for the shareholders.

Chapter 12

The CAPM and Interest Rates

The CAPM is a theoretical model first derived by Treynor (1961a, 1961b), but best known for its independent discovery a few years later by Sharpe (1964), Lintner (1965), and Mossin (1966). The CAPM says that the expected rate of return on a risky asset is equal to the risk-free rate plus some premium for risk; no surprise there.

The Risk Premium

The CAPM is usually written as in Equation 12.1.

$$E(R) = R_F + \beta[E(R_M) - R_F], \qquad (12.1)$$

where R is the return on the asset, R_F is the risk-free rate, R_M is the return on the market portfolio, and $\beta = \frac{cov(R,R_M)}{var(R_M)}$ is the covariance of returns of the asset with the returns of the market portfolio, but taken relative to the variance of the returns of the market portfolio.[1,2]

Let me rewrite the CAPM for some asset A using careful labels in Equation 12.2.

$$E(R_A) = R_F + \overbrace{\underbrace{\beta_A}_{\text{Beta } A} \cdot \underbrace{[E(R_M) - R_F]}_{\text{Market Risk Premium}}}^{\text{Asset } A \text{ Risk Premium}} \qquad (12.2)$$

If we subtract R_F from each side of Equation 12.2,

---

[1] For advanced students: Note that to emphasize two-fund separation, the CAPM relationship may also be rewritten as a convex combination of expected market and risk-free returns as follows: $E(R) = \beta \cdot E(R_M) + (1 - \beta) \cdot R_F$.

[2] Note that the beta $\beta(R, R_M)$ is not the same as the correlation $\rho(R, R_M)$. Can you go back to basic statistics and prove that $\beta(R, R_M) = \rho(R, R_M) \cdot \sigma_R/\sigma_M$?

we get Equation 12.3.

$$\overbrace{E(R_A) - R_F}^{\text{Asset } A \text{ Risk Premium}} = \underbrace{\beta_A}_{\text{Beta } A} \cdot \overbrace{\underbrace{[E(R_M) - R_F]}_{\text{Market Risk Premium}}}^{\text{Asset } A \text{ Risk Premium}} \quad (12.3)$$

So, the risk premium on Asset A is a slice of (or multiple of) the risk premium on the world market portfolio of all risky assets. The CAPM beta is the multiplier. Thus, if the returns R_A of Asset A covary with the returns R_M to give $\beta_A = 1$, then Asset A has the same risk premium as the market as a whole. If the returns R_A covary with the returns R_M to give $\beta_A = 0.5$, then Asset A has half the risk premium of the market as a whole.

The most important part of the CAPM is the form of the individual asset's risk premium (i.e., the RHS of Equation 12.3). This risk premium is compensation for non-diversifiable risk. That is, the CAPM expected return on an asset is the risk-free rate plus compensation for the asset's risk when viewed by the holder of a diversified portfolio.

Let me expand briefly upon this. Suppose I drop a stock with a lot of idiosyncratic (i.e., stock-specific or unique) risk into a diversified portfolio of stocks. When that stock drops into the portfolio, its idiosyncratic risk gets washed out, leaving behind only any covariation in its returns with the returns to the common risk factor (i.e., the world market portfolio of all risky assets). The holder of the diversified portfolio therefore views stocks through risk-tinted spectacles that filter out idiosyncratic risk. That is, to the holder of a diversified portfolio, the only risk in a stock is systematic risk.[3] The expected return on the stock in equilibrium requires a risk premium only for this risk. The functional form of that risk premium (i.e., the RHS of Equation 12.3) falls out of an equilibrium argument that equates supply and demand of risky assets.

The beta term in the CAPM risk premium has attained near-cult status in finance. It is worthwhile pointing out, however, that if you write down a simple market model time series regression equation $R - R_F = \alpha + \beta(R_M - R_F) + \epsilon$, and estimate the beta term using OLS, then the estimate, in the case where R_F is a constant, is none other than $\hat{\beta} = \widehat{cov(R, R_M)} \big/ \widehat{var(R_M)}$. That is, the CAPM

---

[3]Recall that systematic risk in a stock or in a portfolio cannot be removed through diversification. Rather, systematic risk is inherent in the exposure of your stock/portfolio to the economic system as a whole. Systematic risk should be contrasted with stock-specific or idiosyncratic risk that is unique to a stock, and tends to get canceled out when offset against the unique risk in other stocks in a diverse portfolio.

beta is mathematically consistent with the traditional OLS regression coefficient in a market model.

Do not confuse these models; the CAPM is not the market model, and the market model is not the CAPM. The market model is, however, often used to estimate CAPM betas.

Early CAPM literature did not use the symbol β to denote the beta coefficient. We use the beta label now only because it is the second of two coefficients in the standard market model regression estimation; the first coefficient is, of course, called alpha.

CAPM discount rates must compensate for risk and the level of interest rates. Risk includes the risk for that particular stock (represented by β in the CAPM context), and risk for the market as a whole (represented by the market risk premium $[E(R_M)-R_F]$ in the CAPM context). In the CAPM context, the base level of interest rates is the risk-free rate R_F. In practice, all three of these things, beta, market risk premium, and risk-free rate, are time varying. The simple CAPM model we use is, however, a snapshot taken at one point in time. So, we do not place time subscripts on anything.

Mullins (1982, Exhibit V, p. 111) gives a table that ranks industries by CAPM beta. For example, he ranks Air Transport very high with a beta of

1.80, Utilities very low with a beta of 0.60, and Agriculture/Food in the middle with a beta of 1.00.

When Mullins wrote his paper, the U.S. was experiencing a peak in interest rates (followed by the secular decline in rates mentioned on p. 84). Correspondingly, he used interest rates that seem alarmingly high by today's standards: $R_F = 0.10$ and $E(R_M) = 0.19$. He therefore gets very high costs of equity (e.g., $\beta = 1.80$ implies $E(R_E) = 0.262$). Clearly the *level* of interest rates matters very much for discount rates. Nowadays, in the U.S., we typically assume much lower numbers for R_F (see the next section), and we assume a market risk premium $[E(R_M) - R_F]$ between about 5.5% and 7.5%.

Note that although we almost always apply the CAPM to stocks, the CAPM applies to *any* asset (some authors would say any *traded* asset). For example, the CAPM can be used for bonds, but you will almost certainly not see it used for bonds in this class.

The Risk-Free Rate R_F

Another component of the CAPM is the risk-free rate R_F. Now, what exactly is R_F? My question can be interpreted in three different (possibly overlapping) ways. First, what is R_F in the theoretical CAPM model dating back to the 1960s? Second, what number do we use for R_F in the CAPM when doing capital budgeting? Third, what is the economic interpretation of R_F more generally? Let me answer these questions in turn.

1. **R_F in the CAPM:** The original CAPM is a single-period model. That is, it assumes there exists time $t = 0$, say, and time $t = 1$, say. This single period from $t = 0$ to $t = 1$ could be one year, or one day, or one second; it is never specified in the original model. The CAPM describes a required rate of return over that time period. There are two types of assets in the assumed CAPM world: a collection of risky assets that pay off uncertain amounts at time $t = 1$; and, a risk-free asset that gives the same payoff across all possible states of the world at $t = 1$. In this model, R_F is the rate of return on the risk-free asset over the time period. The risk-free asset has no market risk (i.e., no fluctuation in values with different states of the world at $t = 1$). It also has no default risk at $t = 1$ (i.e., there is no possibility that the asset will not return its expected payoff). Thus, we can think of the theoretical R_F as the yield on a Treasury bill (T-bill) issued by

an infinitely credit-worthy government in a world with only two dates on the calendar: now and the maturity date of the T-bill.

2. **R_F Numerically in Capital Budgeting:** Crack (1996) argues that R_F in a capital budgeting implementation of the CAPM should be the long-term T-bond yield less about 100 basis points (recall that there are 100 basis points in one percentage point). This is because of inflation risk (i.e., unanticipated inflation as opposed to anticipated inflation), interest rate risk, and perhaps liquidity risk. The argument given is that we want R_F to be the expected rate of return from rolling short-term T-bills over for, say, 20 years, but the long-term T-bond yield includes this number plus a premium for these various other risks inherent in a 20-year investment.

Why use *long-term* bond yields? Well, I built a spreadsheet containing U.S., U.K., and N.Z. Treasury yield curve data, observed daily over many decades. A graph in the spreadsheet dynamically walks through the data, showing a movie of the evolution of the yield curves (send me an email if you want a copy of the file). Three things stand out in my analysis. First, the curves are typically monotonically upward sloping, but there are periods where they are humped or inverted. Second, the level of the long-term end of the curves changes relatively slowly. Third, the level of the short-term end of the curves moves around more vigorously for much of the sample, and sometimes wags like a happy dog's tail.

So, although we might talk about R_F as being kind of like the yield on rolling over a short-term T-bill, we do not actually want to use short-term rates, because they wag around too much.

Damodaran (2008) says that we should take R_F from the yields on government bonds, but that we should use "strips," not coupon-bearing bonds. (Strips are pure discount bonds. That is, they are zero-coupon bonds that pay off only at maturity.) Damodaran says that we should match the maturity of the strips to the timing of each of the cash flows we wish to discount.

Alternatively, Damodaran (2008) suggests picking a T-bond with duration[4] equal to the dura-

---

[4]Duration is not usually covered explicitly in an introductory finance class. The duration of a bond may be thought of as a measure of sensitivity of bond price to changing interest rates, or as a PV-weighted average of the timing of the cash flows on the bond.

tion of the collective cash flows of the project.

Damodaran (2008) also cautions us against adjusting market numbers that we think are unusual. That is, he says that if you think the R_F you inferred is too low because interest rates are depressed right now, then you should proceed with the low rates. You can then offer any advice you have to your client about the level of the rates outside of the numerical analysis. You can also perform a sensitivity analysis to account for the "unusual" rates.

Finally, Damodaran (2008) gives an extensive discussion of what to do when there is no established government bond market in your country. This overlaps slightly with the next point.

3. **Economic Interpretation of R_F:** Damodaran (2008) argues that R_F is made up of a real risk-free component and an inflation premium as in Equation 12.4.

$$R_F(\text{nominal}) = R_F(\text{real}) + i, \qquad (12.4)$$

where i is the inflation rate.

Damodaran (2008) argues that the real component in Equation 12.4 should be roughly the same from country to country. (So that in the absence of a traded domestic long-term government bond market, anticipated inflation in your domestic market can be added to a real risk-free rate inferred from U.S. Treasuries to build an R_F estimate from scratch.)

What then is that $R_F(\text{real})$ number? That is, what is it conceptually, and how big is it numerically?

Fisher (1930, Chapter IV) argues that one component of the interest rate is the marginal preference for a dollar's worth of early real income over a dollar's worth of deferred real income. He calls this "time preference" or "human impatience." He says that the degree of impatience is the percentage preference for one dollar of immediate certain income over one dollar of certain real income one year from now.

So, we can think of $R_F(\text{real})$ as exactly this compensation for time preference. That is, $R_F(\text{real})$ is compensation for pure human impatience in the absence of risk or inflation.

How big are the components in Equation 12.4? Using U.S. data over the last 90 years or so, my estimate is that $R_F(\text{nominal}) \approx 4.5\%$ per annum, made up of R_F(real) $\approx 1.5\%$ per annum and $i \approx 3\%$ per annum. I base that on average nominal returns to investment in long-term U.S. T-bonds of about 5.5%, the 100 basis point reduction suggested in Crack (1996), and average inflation over the period. Looking forwards, the numbers could be higher or lower depending upon the state of the economy.

Fisher (1930, Chapter IV) goes on to argue that the interest rate as a whole is determined with R_F(real) as a base rate, to which you must make adjustments for risk (i.e., giving a higher interest rate, assuming you are risk averse). He says that if the risk applies to all periods of time in the same way, then it acts as a virtual decrease of income all along the timeline (i.e., risk increases the discount rate applied to future risky income, thereby lowering the PV of that income).

Fisher (1930, Chapter IV) also discusses personal factors like the size and time shape of your income stream, frugality, the wish to leave a bequest, trying to keep up with the fashions, etc. All of which combine to give different people different discount factors at any point in time, and the same person different discount factors through time.

For example, if you are in poverty now, but expect improved income later, then your time preference or impatience is likely quite high; that is, it hurts a lot to give up a dollar now (contributing to a high $R_F(\text{real})$), and you are unlikely to be saving much for the future. Conversely, if you have abundant income now, and expect reduced income later, then time preference or impatience is likely quite low for you now; that is, it does not hurt much to give up a dollar now (contributing to a low $R_F(\text{real})$), and you are likely to be saving for the future.

We can thus think of market interest rates as market-clearing equilibrium prices for money determined by bringing together these subjective views of all market participants.

At the same time, there is also an *objective* element to interest rates. Fisher calls it the "investment opportunity factor" and he attributes it to the "technique of production" (Fisher, 1930, Chapter VII). This is a return to capital, over cost, due to productivity. This productivity is in turn driven by Fisher's maximum present value principal (essentially the CFO's NPV rule applied *en masse*).

So, on the one hand, we can think of interest rates as being determined by a market clearing of the subjective elements (human impatience or time preference for certain real cash flows, inflation, risk, risk aversion, the shape of your income stream, and the other personal factors). On the other hand, we can think about the technique of production (i.e., investment opportunities) in the economy determining interest rates. That is, CFOs chase positive NPV projects, funded by individuals and institutions (in turn ultimately owned by individuals), and the supply of and demand for money to fund these productive endeavors leads to a market clearing price for money—which is the interest rate.

Fisher argues that the afore-mentioned subjective and objective equilibrium interest rates are the same number. That is, we are just looking at different sides of the same coin. On this point, Hirshleifer (1958, pp. 329–330) describes Fisher's greatest contributions in terms of his having considered an equilibrium in the capital markets that includes a clear distinction between exchange opportunities on the one hand (i.e., individuals using the capital markets to balance consumption over time) and production opportunities on the other (i.e., CFOs using NPV/IRR-type rules to add value, acting as agents for individuals)—thus balancing the supply and demand of all market participants. Fisher thus considers capital investment not as an end in itself, but rather as a process of distributing consumption over time (Hirshleifer, 1958, p. 329).

Finally, although it is nowhere modelled explicitly in the standard CAPM, I like to think of the long-run real growth rate in GDP (i.e., taking out the effect of inflation) as being embedded within the interest rate. I think this ties in nicely with Fisher's investment opportunities argument. I think this is embedded within the market risk premium, rather than within the time preference term.[5] This concept is mentioned again on p. 173.

Beyond the CAPM

The remainder of this chapter is for keen finance majors. It goes beyond a first finance class. You may skip this material with impunity if you are an introductory-level student.

---

[5]The U.K. had a 1.9265% geometric average annual real growth rate in GDP from 1830 to 2013 inclusive (Officer and Williamson, 2014) and the U.S. had a 3.7431% geometric average annual real growth rate in GDP from 1790 to 2013 inclusive (Williamson, 2014), but recent growth rates have been much lower.

Fama-French Critique

Many authors have criticized the CAPM. One famous criticism is due to Fama and French (1992, 1993, 2015). They argue that the CAPM fails at explaining returns to stocks and that there exist other risk factors (including a size risk factor and a book-to-market risk factor) that help to explain returns. In other words, when two stocks have different returns, it is not because they have different CAPM betas. On the face of it, this is damning evidence against the CAPM.

Ferguson and Shockley (2003) argue, however, that if you use a popular stock market index to proxy for the CAPM world market portfolio (thus capturing only a slice of the assets in the market portfolio), then you are measuring the independent variable, and beta, with error. So, any economic variables that proxy for this measurement error will serve as instruments that help to explain returns. Ferguson and Shockley (2003) show that the Fama and French (1992, 1993) extra factors would be expected to help explain returns even if the original single-factor CAPM holds. Davidson, Quo, Song, and Tippett (2012) tell a similar story.

Given the arguments in Ferguson and Shockley (2003), any CFO using a stock market index to calculate betas should also augment their CAPM with additional factors (as per the discussion of Graham and Harvey [2001] I gave on p. 144).

Other CAPMs

The original single-factor CAPM is a simple model. It does not contain credit risk, default risk, interest rate risk, liquidity risk, transaction costs, etc. Nothing is time varying in the CAPM because there is only one period. There are several other simple CAPMs that tweak the model slightly. Black's (1972) zero-beta CAPM is probably the best known of these; it allows for the case of no risk-free asset.[6]

In the 1970s two more complicated CAPM models were developed. The first is Merton's (1973) intertemporal capital asset pricing model (ICAPM). It has the same goal as the standard CAPM, modeling expected returns on risky assets, but it does so by asking how investors consume through time,

---

[6]At an introductory level, we might not distinguish between default, downgrade, and credit risks. Default risk is the risk that the bond issuer might fail to pay coupons or principal when due. Downgrade risk is the risk that the credit rating of the bond/issuer is changed by a rating agency, which, in turn, is associated with a change in the yield and the market price of the bond. I think of credit risk as default risk and downgrade risk combined, though other definitions exist.

or defer consumption from now until the future (i.e., intertemporal consumption).

Assuming consumption is funded via wealth generated from investment in securities, investors' concerns about risks to consumption along their future path of consumption should help to explain expected returns now. For example, suppose, unlike the traditional CAPM, that the risk-free rate, or the expected return on the market, or the variance of returns on the market are time varying. Some of these time-varying changes are damaging to future consumption. If there exist securities that have the attractive feature that they will provide higher returns when there is time-varying market-inflicted damage to future consumption, then investors will bid up the prices of those securities, pushing down their expected returns in equilibrium in exchange for the hedging benefit provided. On the other side of the coin, suppose there is time-varying inflation uncertainty. That is, sometimes there will be heavy inflation that worsens the prices of the goods you wish to consume. Again, investors will seek out and bid up the prices of securities that can help hedge these risks, thereby driving down their expected returns, in equilibrium, in exchange for the hedging benefit they provide. You can imagine that stock in a portfolio of gold mining companies might provide a hedge against inflation in general, stock in a portfolio of food producers might provide a hedge against food price rises, and stock in portfolios of various utilities might hedge against water, electricity, and heating oil prices, etc. Merton's ICAPM expresses the expected return on any security as the sum of loadings times expected risk premia on all possible hedge portfolios for these extra market risks (e.g., Bodie, Kane, and Marcus, 2008, p. 316).

The second generalized CAPM is the consumption CAPM (CCAPM). The CCAPM is a model of expected returns as a function of covariation of returns with aggregate growth in consumption (Lucas, 1978; Breeden, 1979). The CCAPM is a single-factor model and quite theoretical.

Although the afore-mentioned long-run real growth rate in GDP is not modelled explicitly in the original CAPM, I think it is reasonable to assume that time-varying growth rates in GDP are correlated with time varying growth rates in aggregate consumption. So, at least in these terms, I think that growth rates in GDP appear in the CCAPM.

Chapter 13

Risk and Return

Over 100 years ago, George Santayana said that those who are ignorant of the past are condemned to repeat it (Santayana, 1905). The late Yogi Berra is reported to have said "The future isn't what it used to be."

We look at risk and return for two reasons: to understand the past (so that we are not surprised by the elements of the past that are likely to reappear in the future), and to model the future. Both of these reasons require appreciation of historical levels of risk and return associated with stocks, bonds, real estate, commodities, currencies, T-bills, and T-bonds. We also need to understand diversification.

(Recall too that we discussed diversification briefly already in the beginning of Chapter 12 when introducing the CAPM.)

The financial markets present many opportunities for investment. My experience is that students stumble over competing concepts of risk associated with these many investments. So, let me give a few selected examples to try to emphasize different types of risks.

- If you buy a U.S. T-bill with face value $1,000,000 that matures in 91 days, then you are almost certainly going to get your promised $1,000,000 in 91 days, and there will be very little that will affect its value in the interim. There is little market price risk and virtually zero default risk. T-bills are liquid, so you can sell them any time during regular trading hours on any trading day (i.e., they have low liquidity risk). Given the fixed payoff in nominal terms, however, you do face a very little purchasing power risk if unexpected inflation flares up and eats some of the real value of your payoff, but you face nothing like the purchasing power risk in a long-term bond.

- Suppose you invest your life savings into the stock of a very small technology company that has never recorded a dime in sales, and that is so new and so small that no analysts follow the company. Then, sure enough, you might double your money in one year, but you might lose it all in three weeks. You face significant market price risk, but you cannot lose more than your initial outlay (assuming you bought the stock with cash, and not using a "margin loan" from your broker). Also, the stock may be quite illiquid. Depending upon the market where the stock trades, there might not be a buyer standing ready to buy the stock from you if you wish to sell; that is liquidity risk. Also, if all your savings are in this one stock, then you are exposed to unnecessary idiosyncratic risk; you could have avoided most of this latter risk by diversifying.

- Suppose you decide that the prices of live cattle are too low given forecast drought conditions. So, you put down an $1,800 margin deposit to go long a live cattle futures contract covering about $50,000 worth of cattle. If prices rise, this leverage multiplies your gains. If, however, prices fall, the leverage means that you can be wiped out very quickly. So, even gently falling prices generate significant market price risk. If futures prices move down by the maximum allowable price change on the exchange (i.e., they "lock limit down"), then trade halts for the day, and you can be stuck in a losing position with no way to get out (another liquidity risk). Prices do not lock limit often, but if it happens several days in a row, you can easily lose much more than your initial margin deposit.

- Suppose you see some slick advertisement for a mutual fund that beat the S&P 500 by 15 percentage points last year. If you invest in the fund, then the fund manager will likely charge you 1% or maybe even 2% or more of your investment value in fees per annum. These fees are not a risk, per se, but they do eat into your investment slowly but surely over time. Also, there is a good chance that the fund manager will underperform the index this year. (On average, the probability that an outperforming fund manager also outperforms its benchmark index the next year is about 60%—only a bit better than a coin toss.) So, you face the risk of underperformance. You also face market price risk. There is also a little liquidity risk, insofar as anyone wishing to buy or sell an open-ended mutual fund usually has to notify the fund company by 10A.M. and then the fund company will execute the trade for you at the close of business that day. So, although there is liquidity, it is not like the liquidity in a "blue chip" (i.e., well established and respectable) stock that you can sell any time during the trading day.

- Suppose you buy some 20-year bonds issued by a well known company, and you plan to hold them until maturity. At the macro-economic level, interest rates have been very low lately, and are expected to rise during the next few years. As the general level of interest rates rises, the PV of the promised fixed coupons and principal on your bond falls. That is, as interest rates rise, bond prices fall, as discussed in Chapter 6.[1] Long-maturity bonds are particularly sensitive to this interest rate risk. At the micro-economic level, you face the downgrade risk that your company might get a credit rating downgrade from a rating agency. Such a downgrade might increase the required return on your bonds (i.e., the yield to maturity) and cause a drop in price. Over the longer run, you also face default risk. For example, what

---

[1]For A+ students: Note that higher interest rates allow you to reinvest your bond coupons at higher rates. Roughly speaking, this reinvestment benefit outweighs the cost of the initial price drop once you hold the bond longer than its initial Macaulay duration.

if the company makes a mistake (e.g., falsifying EPA emissions testing data) that leads to multi-billion dollar costs and possible lawsuits. Your firm might go belly up before you get your principal back.

- Suppose you are very bullish on the S&P 500.[2] So, you buy some twice-levered index exchange-traded funds (ETFs). Over the course of a single day, these funds replicate twice the return on the index quite well. Over multiple days, however, their accumulated return will not track twice the index return so well (Trainor, 2008). So, in addition to roughly double the market price risk, you face a tracking error risk.

- Suppose you buy shares of stock in a small mining company that operates only in a violently dangerous small foreign country that was recently torn by civil war. You likely face significant market risk, driven partly by the risk of more war. Your

---

[2]The market is said to be "tossed up on the horns of the bull," and "clawed down by the bear." We use the words "bull" and "bear" to refer both to market behavior and also to investors holding views about future market behavior. It is less common, but I have also heard the word "crab" used to describe a market whose prices are going neither up nor down, but sideways; this term is not applied to persons.

market risk may also factor in the risk of "expropriation." That is, a new government might take the assets of your firm and kick out all the managers, sending you stock price to zero.

- Buying a house is not, strictly speaking, taking a position in the financial markets. When you use a mortgage, however, to help purchase a house (and most folks do use a mortgage), then you are stepping into the financial markets to access leverage to multiply your initial deposit to the point where you can buy a house. In Chapter 7, I pointed out that millions of Americans still had mortgages that were underwater well after the worst of the global financial crisis was over. Given the leverage involved, it is unwise to extend yourself too much when buying a house. One simple rule of thumb is that if you cannot afford to pay off your house using a 10-year (or shorter) fixed-rate mortgage, then you are likely buying more house than you can afford (Crack, 2017a).

- Finally, suppose that you inherited a lump sum $1,000,000 at Halloween 2007. Suppose you invested it all in a low-fee ETF that replicates the performance of the S&P 500 index of stocks (see the example on p. 186). Suppose you watched your investment steadily lose half its value over the next 16 months (during the beginning of the global financial crisis). Suppose that by the first week of March 2009, you could no longer stand the pain, and you withdrew all your money, having lost a half a million dollars, and vowing never to invest in stocks again. Well, the level of the index climbed 270% (not including the dividends) over the next eight years. If you had not panicked, held onto your investment, and reinvested your dividend income back into the same ETF, it would have been worth over $2,000,000 by July 2017 (with almost $1,850,000 of that value from price appreciation, and the remainder from reinvested dividends). Your inability to sit still and do nothing engendered a market timing risk that created an opportunity cost. Sometimes, *nothing* is the best thing to do in a crisis.

The bottom line is that there are many different types of investments you can make in the financial markets, and they can carry different levels of different sorts of risks. Some investors magnify market risks using leverage, or introduce additional risks by trading at inappropriate times.

Many investors have tolerances for some level of some types of risks, but may have no tolerance for other types of risks. For example, many investors are resigned to the fact that in order to accumulate wealth they have to bear broad market price risk over the long run in the form of holdings in diversified stock mutual funds or retirement savings accounts. Some risks, however, like the idiosyncratic risk exposure from a single stock, can be largely eliminated via diversification. Some risks, like default risk, can be minimized through choice of high-rated bonds only, or through diversification. Similarly, liquidity risk can be reduced by avoiding investment in unproven stock issues.

The majority of investors in the financial markets hold some mixture of stocks and bonds. There are also many alternative investments available, some of which are mentioned in the examples above. Discussing investments that are not stocks leads naturally to a discussion of diversification.

Diversification

Students are often confused by diversification. Let me review some interrelated topics.

I cannot overemphasize how volatile stock prices are. For example, looking at the 86 years in the period 1928–2013, Aswath Damodaran calculates a geometric average return on the S&P 500 of 9.55% per annum including dividends (Damodaran, 2014). That 9.55% per annum sounds quite attractive. There was, however, only one year in that 86-year sample when the S&P 500 return was within 1 percentage point of that average. So, performance-wise, we almost never get an "average" year in stocks.

There were 15 years in that 86-year sample when the S&P 500 return was within plus or minus 5 percentage points of that average—but that interval is 10 percentage points wide! During the other 71 years, the return on the index was outside that 10 percentage-point-wide interval. Stock prices are volatile!

It is important to point out that the above results are for a portfolio containing roughly 500 of the largest (and consequently least volatile) U.S. stocks. So, these results already include a healthy dose of diversification (but only within the equity asset class and only with stocks listed or cross-listed in the U.S.). If I had looked at fewer stocks, or stock with lower "market capitalization" (i.e., the value of all shares outstanding), or only technology stocks, the results would likely have reflected even *more* volatility.

In contrast, the average return on U.S. T-bonds was 4.93% per annum over the 1928–2013 period. The T-bond return was within 1 percentage point of that average 12 times, and within 5 percentage points of that average 52 times out of the 86 years. The average return on U.S. T-bills was 3.53% per annum over this time period. The T-bill return was within 1 percentage point of that average 18 times, and within 5 percentage points of that average 81 times out of the 86 years. Clearly average-performance years are much more likely with T-bonds and T-bills than with stocks.

Corporate bond prices are generally more volatile than T-bond prices but less volatile than stock prices. Combining stocks and corporate bonds can reduce the price risk in your portfolio. So, Jack Bogle (founder of Vanguard Group) recommends the well known rule of thumb that investors hold bonds in the same proportion as their age (e.g., Updegrave, 2011). Thus, a 20-year-old would hold 80% stocks and 20% bonds. (A slightly more aggressive recommendation is a proportion of 120 less your age invested in stocks.)

Of course, true diversification requires holdings beyond U.S. stocks and U.S. bonds, and the financial markets have evolved to offer cheap access to broadly diversified funds that can give you international exposure. For example, Vanguard's Total World Stock Index ETF holds 7,796 stocks from about 50 countries with an expense ratio of only 11 basis points per annum (Vanguard, 2017a).[3] Vanguard's Total International Bond ETF holds 4,486 bonds from about 50 countries with an expense ratio of only 12 basis points per annum (Vanguard, 2017b).[4] These two Vanguard funds, combined with some commodity and real estate holdings, perhaps also via ETFs, would go a long way toward achieving broadly based diversification.

Note, of course, that even if you follow the diversification advice in the previous paragraph, your portfolio will still contain some level of unavoidable systematic risk.

---

[3] Note that if you rank the stock fund's holdings by country, the first half-dozen countries account for 76% of the fund's capitalization (Vanguard, 2017a). You can probably guess which countries these are: U.S. (52.7%), Japan (8.1%), U.K. (6.1%), France (3.1%), Canada (3.0%), Germany (3.0%).

[4] I have noticed that over time the count of holdings in these two Vanguard funds creeps steadily upwards. Meanwhile, their expense ratios decrease slowly in a step function. At the end of July 2017, the Stock fund's assets under management (AUM) was \$11.9b and the Bond fund's AUM was \$84.9b (Vanguard, 2017a, 2017b).

Chapter 14

Market Efficiency

When discussing the efficient market hypothesis (EMH), the word "efficient" means *informationally* efficient. That is, do market prices reflect information? Most students handle efficient markets topics quite well. Let me emphasize just a few points that often go unstated and cause confusion.

In this class, the EMH is usually presented in terms of whether stock market prices reflect information. Some instructors will take an old-school approach (Fama, 1970) where they discuss whether prices should reflect different sets of information (past prices and volumes, public information, or private information). Other instructors take a new-school approach (Fama, 1991) where they look mostly at the speed of the adjustment of prices to new information.

Some academics argue that markets must be efficient, else there would be "money machines" available (i.e., trading strategies that provide consistent abnormal profits). Some practitioners argue that markets must *not* be efficient (or why else do millions of investors demand the services of tens of thousands of fund managers actively trying to beat the performance of their benchmark indices).

The truth is that there is a natural tension at play between prices and information (Grossman and Stiglitz, 1980). Assume for a moment that markets are genuinely informationally efficient. Then stock prices reflect information and nobody has an incentive to collect any information. With no information collection, however, stock prices will soon become informationally inefficient. Conversely, if stock prices are grossly informationally inefficient, then many stocks are mispriced, and there are strong incentives to collect information to correct (and profit from) the mis-pricing. In that case, stock prices will quickly become more efficient.

So, in the real world, practitioners collect information until they think the costs of doing so outweigh the benefits of doing so. In a competitive long-run equilibrium, we might expect, roughly, that most fund managers are smart enough to make just enough money to cover their own fees, leaving investors in their funds with about the same performance on average as if they had not tried to beat the market (Crack, 2017a). In practice, however, fees and costs can leave many investors worse off than if they had not tried to beat the market.

Keep in mind also that taxes, transaction costs, and risk aversion play a part. After all, each of these retards the ability of people to trade on information (Crack, 2017a). So, we do not necessarily expect prices to fully reflect all information all the time.

Indeed, you can think about taxes, transaction costs, and risk aversion as a layer of frictions that sits in the space between investors on the one hand, and the share prices of listed companies on the other.[1] We expect that these frictions will be reflected in rational price formation, insofar as they retard traders' ability to impound information into prices. So, market prices may be determined in

---

[1]I have not seen any other text refer to risk aversion as a "friction." Usually that term is reserved for taxes and transaction costs. Like taxes and transaction costs, however, I view risk aversion as an economic quantity that retards trade. So, I think it is fair to label it as a type of friction here.

a fully rational manner, and yet not be informationally efficient, and the presence of these frictions may mean that the inefficient prices do not provide an exploitable opportunity for consistent abnormal trading profits.

Alternatively, we may view these frictions as creating a buffer zone of stock prices about a fully-efficient stock price (i.e., about the price that would hold in the absence of all such frictions). Given the frictions, however, the inefficient prices within this range/zone are not far enough away from the fully-efficient stock price to be able to be exploited/corrected by traders.

Market inefficiency can also result from internal accounting fraud, external stock price manipulation, overly optimistic traders, etc.

Note, finally, that if stock markets are efficient, and a firm's stock is publicly traded, then SWM is the same thing as stock price maximization. Conversely, if stock markets are not efficient, then these goals differ. Of course, if a company is privately held, maximizing stock price is not feasible because stock price is not observable. In that case, SWM is based on maximizing estimated firm value less value of debt (assuming debt holders are protected against expropriation by stockholders).

Chapter 15

Capital Structure

Capital structure refers to the proportions of debt and equity used to finance a firm. "Capital" refers to financial capital; "structure" refers to the relative proportions.

Let me mention both dividends (covered in more detail in Chapter 16) and capital structure before discussing the latter in more detail. My aim here is to review the topics and clarify competing concepts that typically cause confusion.

Miller and Modigliani (1961) state that in the absence of taxes and other market frictions, the *dividends* a corporation pays do not affect the value of its shares or the returns to investors because the higher the dividend, the less the investor receives in capital appreciation, and vice versa.

An earlier paper (Modigliani and Miller, 1958) says, similarly, that in the absence of taxes and market frictions, the capital structure of the firm is irrelevant to the valuation of the firm.[1] This simple notion of capital structure irrelevance dates back at least to Williams (1938, p. 72).

In the dividend case, with no taxes or transaction costs, an investor is indifferent between receiving dividends from the firm and receiving homemade dividends by selling shares of stock. In the capital structure case, with no taxes or transaction costs, an investor is indifferent between owning shares of stock in a levered firm and borrowing to partially fund the purchase of shares of stock in an unlevered firm. That is, with no taxes or transaction costs, homemade dividends and homemade leverage produce the same results as corporate dividend policy or corporate capital structure policy. In both cases, the homemade policy does not change the value of the company, and thus neither does the corporate policy.

---

[1] Note that both the 1958 and 1961 "MM" papers also discuss the impact of taxes. A correction to MM (1958) appears, however, in MM (1963).

These no-taxes theoretical results are famous and appear in most corporate finance texts. I watched Franco Modigliani present some of these results to an MBA class at MIT in the early 1990s. He stressed (with a mixture of bemusement and annoyance) that these now-famous cases in the absence of taxes and market frictions were never meant to be taken seriously. They were meant only as simplified base cases to which you should then add realistic assumptions to see what happens. That is what we do next.

Over the last 50 years, finance researchers have worked out theories for the relationship between leverage, firm value, and the WACC. This analysis includes costs of financial distress and taxes.[2]

The current state of the optimal capital structure debate is shown in Figure 15.1 (as a function of dollars of debt) and Figure 15.2 (as a function of the debt ratio). I give a bullet-point summary of these arguments after the two plots following.

---

[2]It is above the level of this class, but disagreement still remains over the following: how big the bankruptcy/receivership costs are; the extent to which agency costs lower EBIT as leverage increases; the exact relationship between cost of debt and degree of leverage; the precise effects of personal taxes; and, the impact of dividend imputation.

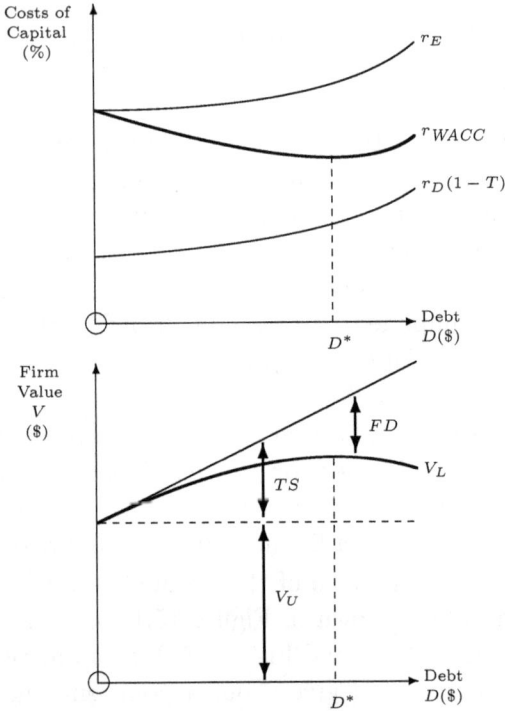

Figure 15.1: Optimal Capital Structure (D)

Hold fixed the physical assets of the company (i.e., the LHS of the balance sheet) and consider a recapitalization. V_L (V_U) is the value of the levered (unlevered) company. $TS = T \times D$ is the PV of the tax shield. FD is the PV of the costs of financial distress. In the lower panel, $V_L = V_U + (T \times D)$ is reduced by FD to give effective V_L. "*" marks the optimum.

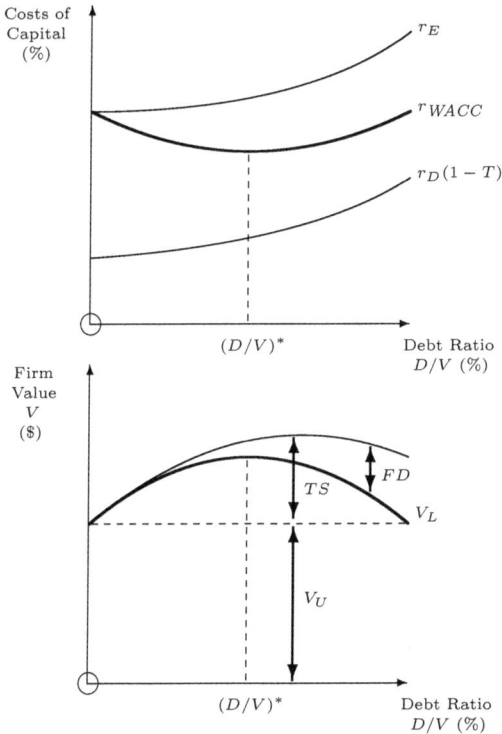

Figure 15.2: Optimal Capital Structure (D/V)

Hold fixed the physical assets of the company (i.e., the LHS of the balance sheet) and consider a recapitalization. V_L (V_U) is the value of the levered (unlevered) company. TS is the PV of the tax shield. FD is the PV of the costs of financial distress. See Equation 15.1 (on p. 204) for one possible/practical definition of the debt ratio. "*" marks the optimum.

- Suppose we hold fixed the physical assets of the company (i.e., the LHS of the balance sheet). Can we somehow generate additional value for our shareholders by altering the capital structure, that is, by altering the relative proportions of debt and equity? If so, then the market value of the assets of the firm will be a function of the capital structure. We can think of this function either as a (cross-sectional) comparison of two firms with identical assets but different capital structures or as a (time series) comparison of the same firm after an announced restructuring of its financing.

- Using no debt is sub-optimal. That is, for the same assets (i.e., changing only the RHS of the balance sheet), the value of the assets of an un-levered firm is less than the value of the assets of a firm with some leverage. This is because the tax-deductibility of debt interest payments adds value to the firm.

- If we issue perpetual debt with face value D, and coupon rate equal to yield r, then the PV of the perpetual stream of future tax deductions is $(T \times C)/r = T \times (r \times D)/r = T \times D$, where C is the perpetual coupon (recall both how to calculate dollar coupons from Chapter 6 and how to value a perpetuity from Chapter 4). This is the value of the debt tax shield in Figures 15.1 and 15.2.

- At first glance, the PV of the tax shield increases as the debt D replaces equity in the capital structure. That is, $V_L = V_U + (T \times D)$, where V_L and V_U are the values of the levered and unlevered firms, respectively (see the uppermost line in the lower panel of Figure 15.1). This assumes the firm pays taxes and can deduct the interest on the debt; not all firms pay taxes (e.g., charities).

- As you increase the proportion of debt in the capital structure, however, you have to worry about whether the firm can generate enough cash flow to "service" the debt (that is, to pay interest when it falls due).

- When the proportion of debt in the capital structure is very high, suppliers might not sell you raw materials for fear that you will not be able to pay for them. Customers might not buy from you for fear that you will not be in business long enough to honor product warranties. Managers may be so busy worrying about cash flow issues that they fail to pay enough attention to running the business properly. Employees may jump ship. The firm might not be able to take on some positive NPV projects because banks might not provide funding in a timely fashion, or at all, for fear that you cannot service the debt. All of these are the "costs of financial distress."

- Let me make this more concrete with a real world example. Chemtura Corporation and its subsidiaries filed for bankruptcy under Chapter 11 of the U.S. bankruptcy code on March 18, 2009.[3]

  In its annual report for that year, Chemtura disclosed risk factors related to its bankruptcy as

---

[3]Under Chapter 11, the entity (e.g., business, individual, married couple) continues to operate, but it attempts to reorganize its debts and make a plan for subsequent exit from bankruptcy. Compare this with a Chapter 7 bankruptcy, under which the entity ceases operations and liquidates its assets. Chemtura was delisted from the NYSE on April 16, 2009 because of the bankruptcy. Bankruptcy is not necessarily forever; Chemtura subsequently exited bankruptcy November 10, 2010, and relisted on the NYSE the next day. In N.Z., individuals can file for bankruptcy, but businesses file instead for one of five different distressed options: Part XIV Compromise; Part XV Arrangement, Amalgamation, or Compromise; Receivership (like Chapter 11); Voluntary Administration; or Liquidation (like Chapter 7).

follows (Chemtura Corporation, 2010):

"...transactions outside the ordinary course of business are subject to the prior approval of the Bankruptcy Court, which may limit our ability to respond timely to certain events or take advantage of certain opportunities.

...A long period of operations under Chapter 11 protection could adversely affect our business and operations. So long as our Chapter 11 cases continue, our senior management will be required to spend a significant amount of time and effort dealing with the reorganization instead of focusing exclusively on our business operations. A prolonged period of operating under Chapter 11 protection may also make it more difficult to attract and retain management and other key personnel necessary to the success and growth of our business. In addition, the longer the Chapter 11 cases continue, the more likely it is that our customers and suppliers will lose confidence in our ability to successfully reorganize our businesses and seek to establish alternative commercial relationships.

Furthermore, so long as the Chapter 11 cases continue, we will be required to incur substantial costs for professional fees and other expenses associated with the administration of the Chapter 11 cases. A prolonged continuation of the Chapter 11 cases may also require us to seek additional financing. If we require additional financing during the Chapter 11 cases and we are unable to obtain the financing on favorable terms or at all, our chances of successfully reorganizing our businesses may be seriously jeopardized, and as a result, any securities in our Company could become devalued or become worthless."

• Continuing with our analysis, we conclude that we have $V_L = V_U + (T \times D) - FD$, where the costs of financial distress, FD, are offset against the PV of the debt tax shield, $(T \times D)$. Note that FD is an increasing function of D. Recall also that D is debt that replaces equity in the capital structure. See Figures 15.1 and 15.2.

• As you increase the proportion of debt in the capital structure, and reduce the proportion of equity, you come to a stage where replacing the next dollar of equity with another dollar of debt will do more harm via the above-mentioned costs of financial distress than it does good via the increased debt tax shield. So, there is an optimal level of debt in the capital structure. At this optimum, more debt would be bad (i.e., FD rises by more than $T \times D$) and less debt would be bad (i.e., $T \times D$ falls by more than FD falls). At this optimum, the value of the assets of the firm are maximized. This is shown in the lower panels of Figures 15.1 and 15.2.

- A similar argument applies to the costs of capital, as in the upper panels of Figures 15.1 and 15.2. As you increase the proportion of debt in the capital structure, and reduce the proportion of equity, the cost of debt slowly rises, and so too does the cost of equity. The WACC lowers at first (because debt financing is cheaper than equity financing and you are replacing equity with debt), but eventually rising costs of debt and rising costs of equity drive up the WACC. At the optimum where the value of the assets of the firm is maximized, the WACC is minimized.

- Note, however, that if you announce that you are about to issue bonds to buy back stock in an all-equity firm, then equity prices will shoot up in anticipation of the benefits. So, you will have to pay the premium earned (i.e., tax shield less costs of financial distress) to exiting shareholders as well as creating it for the remaining shareholders.

For example, if an all-equity firm has $100M of equity, and an optimal target capital structure of 50:50 (at which the assets in place would be worth, say, $120M), then you cannot just issue $50M of bonds and buy back half the equity for $50M; this does not make sense. Rather, after the announcement, you have to issue $60M of bonds and buy back half the equity for $60M.

- Note that the only firms likely to be sitting at the far right of Figure 15.1 or Figure 15.2 are ones whose earnings prospects have fallen substantially since the time when their debt was issued, because new lenders are unlikely to willingly lend to a company in such dire straits (see Miller and Modigliani, 1961, p. 275).

- Finally, in practice, and as mentioned in the extract from the Chemtura annual report, the rise in the cost of debt might instead materialize as increasingly stringent restrictions imposed by the creditors on the company's operations and financing, ultimately leading to an inability to borrow at all in the institutional space. Hirshleifer (1958, p. 339) refers to this inability to borrow as a "Scitovsky situation." See also Miller and Modigliani (1961, p. 273).

Do firms actually behave as if there is an optimal capital structure? The Graham and Harvey (2001) survey of CFOs finds that 81% of firms say they have a target debt ratio (for 10% it is very strict; for 34% it is somewhat tight; and for 37% it is flexible); the other 19% have no target debt ratio. The target debt ratios are stricter at large firms, firms with investment-grade debt, and regulated firms (e.g., utilities). So, yes, many firms have an optimal target debt ratio.

There is significant variation in debt ratios across industry groups (Berk and DeMarzo, 2007, p. 479). That is because the optimal level of debt is a function of stability of cash flows (e.g., a firm with very volatile cash flows should not have high debt because of the likelihood of bankruptcy). Stability of cash flows is influenced negatively by business risk (i.e., risk to the cash flows themselves rather than any of the market risks we discussed previously), positively by transparency of the business (e.g., a higher proportion of tangible assets), and positively by good corporate governance (i.e., the processes by which the firm is managed and their alignment with stakeholder interests).

The phrase "debt ratio" means different things to different people. There are many different ways to define the numerator and the denominator in the debt ratio. So, what sort of debt ratios are we talking about here? Let us pin down one definition, and then explore typical magnitudes.

de Jong, Kabir, and Nguyen (2008) define their debt ratio as the book value of long-term debt over the market value of total assets, where the market value of total assets is the book value of total assets less the book value of equity plus the market value of equity, as in Equation 15.1.

$$
\begin{aligned}
\text{Debt Ratio} &= \frac{BV(LTD)}{MV(TA)} \\
&= \frac{BV(LTD)}{BV(TA) - BV(E) + MV(E)}
\end{aligned}
$$

(15.1)

de Jong, Kabir, and Nguyen report an average debt ratio of 12.9% (median 11.9%) across 11,845 firms in 42 countries. The average for the U.S. was 14.4% (median 9.3%) in their study.

Using the definition of debt ratio in Equation 15.1, in the 30 stocks of the Dow Jones Industrial Average at the end of the third quarter of 2015, I find an average debt ratio of 11.5% (median 11.1%). The maximum was 26.0% (for Verizon); the minimum was 0% (for Visa). Looking at 498 of the 505 stocks in the S&P 500 index at the end of the third quarter of 2015 (seven stocks had missing values on some inputs), I find an average debt ratio of 15.4% (median 12.4%). The maximum was 93.0% (for Navient); the minimum was 0% (for 15 firms). My numbers seem consistent with de Jong, Kabir, and Nguyen (2008).[4]

In summary, many firms have target debt ratios, global averages using Equation 15.1 are around 10%–15%, but there is much variation.

Finally, for finance majors, let me mention the intersection of optimal capital structure (this chapter), FCF estimation (Chapter 9), and costs of capital (Chapter 10). We said on p. 130 that for FCF estimation, the focus is on the LHS (i.e., the asset side) of the balance sheet without regard to the

---

[4]Using instead Debt Ratio = $BV(LTD)/BV(TA)$ (i.e., a book-based measure of the debt ratio), gives ratios roughly double those reported using the market value measure in Equation 15.1. For example, for the 30 Dow stocks, the average book-based debt ratio is then 20.8%, the median is 20.3%, and the maximum is 54.6% (for McDonald's). For 499 of the 505 S&P 500 stocks, the average book-based debt ratio is then 25.5%, the median is 23.8%, and the maximum is 133.0% (for Cablevision Systems; yes, that is a negative book value of equity). The differences between the two measures of debt ratio are driven by differences between the book value of equity and the market value of equity.

RHS (i.e., the financing side). In fact, when we use prudent weights in the WACC (as mentioned on p. 148), these weights should, in theory, be the optimal/target weights discussed in this chapter. At a prudent level of financing, however, the FCFs are likely to include some costs of financial distress, purely as a consequence of normal business activity. These financial distress costs may be quite minor. Thus the RHS of the balance sheet *does* have an impact on the FCF, but only insofar as financial distress drives *operating* cash flows. The debt tax shield, however, is not accounted for in the FCF, but rather it appears via the use of the after-tax cost of debt appearing in the WACC—because the debt tax shield is driven by financing, not by operations. If we also, incorrectly, include the debt tax shield in the FCF, then we are double counting the tax-benefit of debt, as mentioned on p. 132.

Chapter 16

Dividends

Dividend policy is a company's decision whether to pay a dividend or not, and if it pays one, how much it will be and what form it will take.

Dividends have always been a little mysterious. For example, Fischer Black wrote a four-page paper titled "The Dividend Puzzle" that walks through reasons why corporations pay dividends, and why investors like them. He concludes with: "What should the individual investor do about dividends in his portfolio? We don't know. What should the corporation do about dividend policy? We don't know (Black, 1976, p. 11)"

Given the puzzle, let me walk through some simple arguments regarding dividends and let me try to address some common points of confusion.

The dividend yield on a stock is the cash dividends paid over a year divided by the price of the stock. On p. 96 we noted that, in practice, the dividends used in this calculation are usually the trailing 12-month dividends (though forecast dividends are used in the dividend yield calculation in the Gordon-Shapiro model on p. 96).

The average dividend yield on the S&P 500 portfolio over the 50 years from mid-1963 to mid-2013 was 3.1%. That sounds like a small number. Consider, however, a tax-free investor (e.g., a pension fund) who made a lump sum investment into the S&P 500 stocks mid-1963, and who reinvested those dividends back into the stocks as they were paid over the following 50 years. In this case, the reinvested dividends account for 79% (i.e., very nearly *four-fifths*) of the ending wealth of the investor over that 50-year period (Crack, 2017a). So, dividends are in fact very important!

Why do companies pay cash dividends? Surely, a stock that is worthwhile owning must have something more worthwhile to do with its earnings than just handing them back to you as a cash dividend— typically with a tax obligation. So, why do so many companies do exactly that? (I give some percentages in a few pages.)

Two reasons for paying dividends come immediately to mind. First, a company might not have a good use for the retained earnings. For example, in 2014, 98% of voting Berkshire Hathaway investors voted in favor of reinvesting all earnings and *not* paying a dividend (Buffett, 2014, p. 38). Indeed, the "Buffett System" explicitly states that Berkshire will not pay dividends as long as each dollar of retained earnings generates more than a dollar of market value for investors (Buffett, 2014, p. 40). Nevertheless, even Warren Buffett acknowledges that some time, between 10 and 20 years in the future, Berkshire will be so large that it will be unable to intelligently reinvest all its earnings and will either pay a dividend or, if the stock is selling below intrinsic value, buy back its stock (Buffett, 2014, p. 36).

Second, investors like dividends. The old-fashioned "bird-in-the-hand" argument says that investors do not trust their agents (i.e., the firm's managers) to turn the current (i.e., certain) cash flows into future (i.e., uncertain) cash flows (Gordon, 1963). So, getting a cash dividend payment back from the firm is like getting back $10 of the

$50 you lent to a potentially untrustworthy acquaintance. That begs the question, though, because if you bought $50 worth of stock, what is to stop you selling $10 of it and making your own dividend (like the Miller and Modigliani [1961] argument mentioned in Chapter 15)? Also, if you do not trust the managers, why do you own the stock they manage upon your behalf in the first place?

Beyond the above discussion, I think companies pay dividends (or do not pay dividends) for the following reasons:

- Dividends are used by companies as a signaling mechanism regarding prospects for sustainable future earnings growth. Indeed, if a company initiates dividend payments, its stock price typically goes up, and if it cuts (or omits entirely) its dividends, its stock price usually goes down (Asquith and Mullins, 1983; Healy and Palepu, 1988). That is because investors assume that behind any changing dividend is a management forecast of changing future earnings. Management have these earnings forecast signals uppermost in their minds, and they know what happens to stock prices when dividends change, so they are very mindful of the pattern and continuity of past dividends (Baker and Powell, 2000).

- Some real estate investment trusts (REITs; they trade like stocks on the stock exchange) can avoid paying any taxes if they pay out at least 90% of their earnings as dividends. So, they become regular payers of dividends. On the other side of the coin, some trusts and endowments are prohibited from spending principal, and thus they form a clientele that likes receiving dividends.

- In some countries at some times, dividends are taxed at a lower rate than long-term capital gains. For example, dividends were tax exempt in the U.S. during 1913–1935 (CRS, 2014). In these cases, investors may prefer cash dividends to the homemade dividends they can get from selling their stock. Note that such marginal tax rate motivations do not apply to U.S./U.K. pension funds (because they typically pay no taxes on the money they manage).

- Conversely, note that debt covenants may limit the amount that a firm is able to pay out in dividends, so as not to enrich stockholders at debtholder expense.

- Note that young/growing firms often pay no dividends, preferring to keep the internal capital to fund growth. So, for example, the proportion of firms that pay dividends is roughly 45% on the NYSE, 27% on Nasdaq, and only 7% on the OTC Bulletin Board (Crack, 2017a). These proportions are in line with the types of firms that traditionally trade on these venues (e.g., older and larger firms on the NYSE versus younger and higher-growth firms on the Nasdaq).

- Finally, some academics argue that firms use dividend payouts to reduce the possibility of overinvestment by management. That is, left to their own devices, managers may spend too much on CAPEX, destroying shareholder wealth by over-investing into negative NPV pet projects. This is an agency cost to shareholders. When shareholders vote to force managers to pay dividends, they may be reducing this agency conflict (Farre-Mensa, Michaely, and Schmalz, 2014). Ultimately, I think that this could help to explain the bird-in-the-hand argument. Note, however, that Baker and Powell (2000) survey CFOs from 197 NYSE firms, and ask them about determinants of dividend policy. Baker and Powell rank the top 20 determinants, and, although the agency notion is popular with academics, paying dividends "instead of undertaking risky reinvestment" is ranked by CFOs at a very lowly 18 out of 20.

Dividends as Corporate Actions

Paying a dividend is one example of a corporate action. More generally, a corporate action is an important event in the life of a company. It usually has a direct impact on the structure of the ownership rights of the shareholders. Corporate actions are usually agreed upon by the board of directors and voted on by the shareholders. Examples include dividends, acquisitions, liquidations, mergers, rights issues, spin-offs, stock splits, and takeovers. Let me mention a few corporate actions related to dividends:

- A cash dividend: A cash payment from the company to you that does not require you to give up any of your stock.

- A dividend reinvestment plan (DRIP): A scheme that allows you to convert some or all of your cash dividends into new shares of stock. Some DRIP schemes are run by the company, and others are run by outside entities (e.g., brokerage houses).

- A repurchase (or "buy back"): The company gives you a cash payment and you give up some or all of your stock.

- A rights issue: To raise new capital, a company grants stockholders the right to acquire newly issued stock, often at a slight discount from recent prices. The rights can be detached from the stock and sold separately in the marketplace. Rights issues are rare in the U.S., but common in N.Z.

- Diluting transactions where no new capital is raised. Although cosmetic, all but the last one in the following list signal a "vote of confidence," and they lower stock price (which some folks argue may improve liquidity in the stock):

  ○ A stock dividend: Additional shares are issued to you without changing the par value of existing shares. There is a transfer from retained earnings to permanent capital. Often, but not always, there is an increase in the count of shares of fewer than 25% (e.g., a 10% stock dividend). The Nike example a page forward is a counter example.

  ○ A stock split: Additional shares are issued to you with a change in par value of existing shares. There is no change in retained earnings. There is typically an increase in the count of shares of more than 25% (e.g., a 2-for-1 split, where the count of shares doubles, the par value of each share halves, and the market price per share roughly halves).

- A bonus issue (also called a "capitalization issue" or "scrip issue"): Like a stock dividend, this is an accounting move of money from one account that belongs to the shareholders to another account that belongs to the shareholders.

- Finally, and conversely, a reverse split (e.g., a 1-for-10 split) can lift a penny stock's price.

In practice, some of the above-mentioned corporate actions can be combined. For example, after the close of trade on November 19, 2015, Nike announced that it planned to repurchase $12 billion worth of its stock over the coming four years, conduct a 2-for-1 stock split executed as a 100% stock dividend the following month, and increase its quarterly dividend from 28 cents per share to 32 cents per share (Townsend, 2015). The stock price reacted by jumping a respectable 5.5% to close at $132.65 per share in New York on November 20, 2015. This brought Nike's market capitalization to roughly $113 billion.

(Finance majors might like to note that Nike was the fourth-highest priced stock of the 30 stocks in the Dow Jones Industrial Average at that time.

The Dow-30 index is a little unusual in that the index level is a *price*-weighted average of the prices of the member stocks. On the day of the 5.5% jump in Nike's stock price, that jump was responsible for one quarter of a 150-point opening surge in the Dow-30. That was a jump of just under one percent in the index. After the 2-for-1 split, however, Nike dropped to 21st position in the Dow-30 when ranked on price, and the influence of its price on the level of the Dow dropped dramatically.)

Let me give one more example of combined corporate actions that include a change in dividend policy. This one, however, has quite the opposite spin of the Nike example. On December 8, 2015, Anglo American (one of the world's largest mining companies, with interests in coal, metals, diamonds, etc.), shocked financial markets by announcing that it would sell off about 60% of its assets, cut 60% of its workforce, drastically reduce CAPEX, and omit its dividend for the second half of 2015 and for 2016 (Biesheuvel, 2015). The stock price dropped 12% in London on the news, closing at a historic low of 323.65 pence per share, down roughly 70% on the year, and down about 80% over the previous 18 months. The stock fell yet another 10% over the following week! Anglo's corporate actions followed a collapse in commodity prices, triggered partly by a reduction in Chinese demand (Smith, 2015).

Note that in neither the Nike case nor the Anglo American case was the change in dividend policy directly responsible for the stock price change. Rather, the stock price change was in response to changes in the underlying prospects for sustainable future earnings growth, as signaled through the change in dividend policy and other corporate actions.

Dividend Imputation

Dividend imputation is supposed to reduce or eliminate double taxation of dividends. (This section can be safely skipped over by most U.S. students.)

Dividend imputation is often confusing. Let me explain it in simple terms. Suppose you own shares of a U.S. stock that has good healthy positive earnings. Well, whose earnings are those? Surely, the earnings (or at least a slice of them) are *your* earnings, because you are, after all, the owner of the company (or at least the owner of a slice of the company). So, when the company pays corporate income tax on those earnings to the Internal Revenue Service (IRS), whose taxes is it paying? The answer is that it is paying your taxes to the IRS on your behalf; this is nothing other than taxes on your slice of the earnings from your slice of the firm that you own. If, out of after-tax earnings, the company then pays you a dividend, the IRS then requires you to pay taxes on that dividend also.

You could make the argument, however, that you already paid your taxes on those earnings, and that the IRS has no right to tax you again. You could refuse to pay the taxes and you could argue all the way to your jail cell that this is double taxation of the earnings made by the company you own a slice of, and that this tax is a disincentive for companies to pay dividends, and a disincentive for you to own stock. If this was a sole proprietorship, rather than a corporation, for example, your earnings from the sole proprietorship would be taxed only once at the personal level.[1]

Now, sure enough, the IRS can make the counter-argument that, in fact, the company is a legal entity in its own right, and that that entity is taxed on its income, and that you are then taxed on your income paid to you by that entity. That is per-

---

[1]Note that some small domestic U.S. corporations can avoid double taxation of earnings by forming an "S corporation" (IRS, 2016).

fectly correct, but that is not how some countries think about it.

In Australia and N.Z., the tax authorities have taken the point of view that if the company has paid taxes on your slice of earnings already, and then paid you a dividend out of the after-tax earnings, then you should declare the pre-tax dividend as a gross dividend on your personal income tax return, combine that gross dividend with other gross taxable income, calculate your taxes due in the normal way, and then offset against those taxes any amount already paid by the company to the tax authority on your behalf. (Germany and France also had dividend imputation systems, but removed them in the early 2000s.)

That is, you get to declare the pre-tax gross dividend as a part of your taxable income (rather than the after-tax dividend you would declare in the U.S.), and you get a tax credit to offset against the tax due (rather than getting no tax credit in the U.S.). The tax credit is called a "dividend imputation tax credit" or a "dividend franking tax credit," or something similar.

The dividend imputation tax credit is not always equal to the amount of personal income tax you owe on the dividend. If you are in a higher tax bracket than the firm, you will owe additional taxes (which may already have been additionally withheld by the firm and sent to the tax authority on your personal behalf). Conversely, if you are in a lower tax bracket than the firm, you may get a tax refund, or you can redirect the taxes already paid on your behalf toward some other tax due. Sometimes the company issues only a partial imputation credit because it did not pay taxes at the full rate. If the company had a loss, and paid no taxes, but still paid a dividend, then it may issue no imputation tax credit, because it paid no taxes on your behalf. The bottom line is that dividend imputation is supposed to reduce or eliminate double taxation of dividends, so it kicks in only when the company actually pays taxes, and only in the countries adopting this system.

Conclusion

Let me summarize my advice. Look back through the book, or use the index to find more detail on any of these main points.

- Follow the Lincoln Approach (p. 4). Embrace the material without fear and it will become clear.

- Almost every topic in this book is related in some way to almost every other topic in this book. You should actively look for linkages between the topics, rather than thinking about the topics as residing in separate silos.

- Be prepared to use the dinner party rule discussed on p. 31 to solve for any variable in an equation in terms of any other. It is not always possible to do so (e.g., you cannot solve the general PV of an annuity formula, Equation 4.1, explicitly for r).

- Learn to use the memories of your calculator to store intermediate answers, so as not to lose any decimal places.

- Use the safe strategy rules to solve numerical problems: draw a timeline, label it, have a guess, write down the formula algebraically, fill in the numbers, confirm the answer is in the ball park, and double-check with a simpler formula where possible.

- Always be on the lookout for annuities. Do not accidentally discount annuities term-by-term, because it is time consuming and error prone.

- Note that although the actions of inflating and deflating appear mechanically similar to the actions of compounding and discounting, they are not the same. We usually compound at rate r and inflate at rate i, where $r = i + $ (other stuff).

- We pointed out exactly what the IRR rule does and does not do. It is a simple rule that agrees with the NPV rule for a single project with standard cash flows (i.e., a project with a single cash outflow followed by subsequent cash inflows), and a constant discount rate. In almost every other situation, and especially with competing projects, the IRR rule cannot be used to make decisions. The IRR rule does, however, sometimes act as a lens through which you can view the relative scale or relative timing of cash flows to competing projects. Osborne (2010, 2014) provides a definitive reconciliation of the NPV and IRR rules.

- When calculating unlevered FCF (e.g., for an NPV calculation), we focus on the LHS (i.e., asset side) of the balance sheet and ignore the RHS (i.e., financing side) of the balance sheet. When discounting the FCF, however, we do adjust the cost of debt (as part of the WACC) to account for the tax-deductibility of interest.

- When discussing optimal capital structure, we focus first on the LHS of the balance sheet, and conclude that in the absence of taxes, capital structure is irrelevant for firm value. We then introduce taxes and costs of financial distress and conclude that holding fixed the assets of the firm, the RHS of the balance sheet has an impact on value (positively for the debt tax shield and negatively for costs of financial distress). The tradeoff leads to an optimal capital structure that maximizes firm value and minimizes the WACC.

- We introduced the CAPM as a model of expected returns. It says simply that the expected return on an asset is the risk-free rate plus a premium for risk. We argued that this premium is viewed from the perspective of a diversified investor who cares only about systematic risk.

- We spent more time discussing inflation and interest rates than many texts. This is because the concepts cause great confusion, partly because they are rarely explained well.

- On the EMH front, we focused attention on two fronts. First, the tension between prices and information that drives some market participants to collect information that leads to more informationally efficient prices. Second, the tension between efficient prices on the one hand, and frictions (i.e., taxes, transactions costs and risk aversion) on the other hand, where these frictions can be expected to retard the ability of market participants to trade upon information, thereby producing seemingly less efficient (but rationally justified) market prices, with no opportunities for unusual trading profits.

- We discussed many different aspects of dividend policy. Be sure to review the arguments for and against paying dividends, but accept that dividends have always been a little mysterious.

- Let me finish by saying that barring a health emergency or a security alert, there is no good reason for leaving an exam early. If you have any free time at the end of the exam, then you should use it to double-check all your quantitative answers (e.g., Did you use all the elements of the safe strategies I recommended?). If you still have time left after doing that, then reread all qualitative answers.

Finally, let me repeat my request from the beginning of the book. If after reading this book and making an honest effort with the material, you find that your understanding and your grades improve, then please go to `Amazon.com` and leave a positive review for this book, so that other people may similarly benefit from it. Just type the ISBN number from the back cover into Amazon's Web site and then click on the box labeled "Write a customer review." Thank you.

References

Asquith, Paul and David W. Mullins, Jr., 1983, "The Impact of Initiating Dividend Payments on Shareholders' Wealth," *The Journal of Business*, Vol. 56 No. 1, (January), pp. 77–96.

Baker, H. Kent and Gary E. Powell, 2000, "Determinants of Corporate Dividend Policy: A Survey of NYSE Firms," *Financial Practice and Education*, Vol. 10 No. 1, (Spring/Summer, March), pp. 29–40.

Berk, Jonathan and Peter DeMarzo, 2007, *Corporate Finance*, Pearson International Edition: Boston, MA.

Bernstein, Asaf, 2016, "Household Debt Overhang and Labor Supply," Working Paper, Massachusetts Institute of Technology, (January), 67pp.

Biesheuvel, Thomas, 2015, "Anglo to Shrink by Two-Thirds, End Dividends as Metals Plunge," Available at: http://www.bloomberg.com/news/articles/2015-12-08/anglo-scraps-dividend-to-save-cash-as-commodities-tumble (dated December 8, 2015; downloaded December 2015).

Binder, John J. and Chaput, J. Scott, 1996, "A Positive Analysis of Corporate Capital Budgeting Practices," *Review of Quantitative Finance and Accounting*, Vol. 6 No. 3, (May), pp. 245–257.

BKFS, 2016, "Black Knight's February Mortgage Monitor," Black Knight Financial Services Press Release, Available at www.bkfs.com (dated April 4, 2016; downloaded July 2016).

Black, Fischer, 1972, "Capital Market Equilibrium with Restricted Borrowing," *The Journal of Business*, Vol. 45 No. 3, (July), pp. 444–455.

Black, Fischer, 1976, "The Dividend Puzzle," *The Journal of Portfolio Management*, Vol. 2 No. 2, (Winter), pp. 5–8.

BLS, 2015, "Consumer Price Index: Frequently Asked Questions (FAQs)," Available at: http://www.bls.gov/cpi/cpifaq.htm (dated July 24, 2015; downloaded October 2015).

Bodie, Zvi, Alex Kane, and Alan J. Marcus, 2008, *Investments*, Seventh Ed., McGraw-Hill: Boston, MA.

Brealey, Richard A., and Stewart C. Myers, 1991, *Principles of Corporate Finance*, Fourth Edition, McGraw-Hill: New York, NY.

Breeden, Douglas T., 1979, "An Intertemporal Asset

Pricing Model with Stochastic Consumption and Investment Opportunities," *Journal of Financial Economics*, Vol. 7 No. 3, (September), pp.265-296.

Buffett, Warren, 2014, *2014 Letter to Shareholders of Berkshire Hathaway*, Available at: http://berkshirehathaway.com/letters/2014ltr.pdf

Burrell, O.K., 1960, "A Mathematical Approach to Growth Stock Valuation," *The Financial Analysts Journal*, Vol. 16 No. 3, (May-June), pp. 69–72, 75, 76.

Chemtura Corporation, 2010, U.S. Securities and Exchange Commission, Form 10-K, Annual Report For the fiscal year ended December 31, 2009, Available at: http://investor.chemtura.com/ (dated March 12, 2010; downloaded November 2015).

Crack, Timothy Falcon, 1996, "DCF and Free Cash Flow: Notes from a Financial Management Course Taught by Kevin Rock at MIT in 1996," 6pp.

Crack, Timothy Falcon, 2017a, *Foundations for Scientific Investing: Capital Markets Intuition and Critical Thinking Skills*, Seventh Edition. See the advertisement at the end of this book.

Crack, Timothy Falcon, 2017b, *Basic Black-Scholes: Option Pricing and Trading.* Revised Fourth Edition. See the advertisement at the end of this book.

Crack, Timothy Falcon, and Helen M. Roberts, 2018, "Building Modular Dividend Discount Models Using the 'Super Annuity Formula'," Working Paper, Otago University, (March 12), 23pp.

CRS, 2014, "The Taxation of Dividends: Background and Overview," *Congressional Research Service*, CRS Report R43418, Prepared for Members of Congress, March 10, 29pp.

Damodaran, Aswath, 2008, "What is the Riskfree Rate? A Search for the Basic Building Block," Working Paper, NYU, (December), 33pp.

Damodaran, Aswath, 2012, *Investment Valuation: Tools and Techniques for Determining the Value of Any Asset*, Third Edition, John Wiley & Sons: Hoboken, NJ.

Damodaran, Aswath, 2014, EXCEL file histretSP.xls, Available at: http://pages.stern.nyu.edu/ adamodar/ (downloaded July 2014).

Davidson, Ian, Qian Quo, Xiaojing Song, and Mark Tippett, 2012, "Constructing Asset Pricing Models With Specific Factor Loadings," *Abacus*, Vol. 48 No. 2, (June), pp. 199–213.

de Jong, Abe, Rezaul Kabir, Thuy Thu Nguyen, 2008, "Capital Structure Around The World: The Roles of Firm- and Country-Specific Determinants," *Journal of Banking and Finance*, Vo. 32 No. 9, (September), pp. 1954–1969.

DMO, 2017, "Gilt Market," UK Government Debt Management Office, Available at:

http://www.dmo.gov.uk/index.aspx?page=gilts/
about_gilts (dated 2017; downloaded July 2017).

Fama, Eugene F., 1970, "Efficient Capital Markets: A
Review of Theory and Empirical Work," *The Journal
of Finance*, Vol. 25 No. 2, (May), pp. 383–417.

Fama, Eugene F., 1991, "Efficient Capital Markets: II,"
The Journal of Finance, Vol. 46 No. 5, (December),
pp. 1575–1617.

Fama, Eugene F., and Kenneth R. French, 1992, "The
Cross-Section of Expected Stock Returns," *The Journal of Finance*, Vol. 47 No. 2, (June), pp. 427–465.

Fama, Eugene F., and Kenneth R. French, 1993,
"Common Risk Factors in the Returns on Stocks
and Bonds," *Journal of Financial Economics*, Vol. 33
No. 1, (February), pp. 3–56.

Fama, Eugene F. and Kenneth R. French, 2015, "A
Five-Factor Asset Pricing Model," *Journal of Financial Economics*, Vol. 116 No. 1, (April), pp. 1–22.

Farre-Mensa, Joan, Roni Michaely, and Martin
Schmalz, 2014, "Payout Policy," *Annual Review of Financial Economics*, Vol. 6, (December), pp. 75–134,
edited by Andrew W. Lo and Robert C. Merton. Palo
Alto, CA.

Ferguson, Michael F., and Richard L. Shockley, 2003,
"Equilibrium Anomalies," *The Journal of Finance*,
Vol. 58 No. 6, (December), pp. 2549–2580.

Fisher, Irving, 1930, *The Theory of Interest: As Determined by Impatience to Spend Income and Opportunity to Invest it*, Macmillan: New York, NY.

Gordon, Myron J., and Eli Shapiro, 1956, "Capital Equipment Analysis: The Required Rate of Profit," *Management Science*, Vol. 3 No. 1, (October), pp. 102–110.

Gordon, Myron J., 1963, "Optimal Investment and Financing Policy," *The Journal of Finance*, Vol. 18 No. 2, (May), pp. 264–272.

Graham, Benjamin, 2006, *The Intelligent Investor: The Definitive Book on Value Investing*, Revised Edition, Harper Collins: New York, NY. (Originally published in 1949.)

Graham, Benjamin and David Dodd, 1934, *Security Analysis: The Classic 1934 Edition*, McGraw-Hill: New York, NY.

Graham, John R., and Campbell R. Harvey, 2001, "The Theory and Practice of Corporate Finance: Evidence from the Field," *Journal of Financial Economics*, Vol. 60 No. 2-3, (May), pp. 187–243.

Grossman, Sanford J., and Joseph E. Stiglitz, 1980, "On the Impossibility of Informationally Efficient Markets," *American Economic Review*, Vol. 70 No. 3, (June), pp. 393–408.

Healy, Paul M., and Krishna G. Palepu, 1988, "Earnings Information Conveyed by Dividend Initiations and Omissions," *Journal of Financial Economics*, Vol. 21 No. 2, (September), pp. 149–175.

Hirshleifer, J., 1958, On the Theory of Optimal Investment Decision, *Journal of Political Economy*, Vol. 66 No. 4, (August), pp. 329–352.

IRS, 2016, "S Corporations," Avaiable at: https://www.irs.gov/businesses/small-businesses-self-employed/s-corporations (dated August 1, 2016; downloaded September 2016).

Jensen, Michael C., 2002, "Value Maximization, Stakeholder Theory, and the Corporate Objective Function," *Business Ethics Quarterly*, Vol. 12 No. 2, (April), pp. 235–256.

Lintner, John, 1965, "Security Prices, Risk, and Maximal Gains from Diversification," *The Journal of Finance*, Vol. 20 No. 4 (December), pp. 587–615.

Lucas, Robert E., Jr., 1978, "Asset Prices in an Exchange Economy," *Econometrica*, Vol. 46 No. 6, (November), pp. 1429–1445.

Merton, Robert C., 1973, "An Intertemporal Capital Asset Pricing Model," *Econometrica*, Vol. 41 No. 5, (September), pp. 867–887.

Miller, Merton H., and Franco Modigliani, 1961, "Dividend Policy, Growth and the Valuation of Shares," *Journal of Business*, Vol. 34 No. 4, (October), pp. 411–433.

Modigliani, Franco, and Merton H. Miller, 1958, "The Cost of Capital, Corporation Finance and the Theory of Investment," *The American Economic Review*, Vol. 48 No. 3, (June), pp. 261–297.

Modigliani, Franco, and Merton H. Miller, 1963, "Corporate Income Taxes and the Cost of Capital: A Correction," *The American Economic Review*, Vol. 53 No. 3, (June), pp. 433–443.

Mossin, Jan, 1966, "Equilibrium in a Capital Asset Market," *Econometrica*, Vol. 34 No. 4 (October), pp. 768–783.

Mullins, David W., 1982, "Does the Capital Asset Pricing Model Work?," *Harvard Business Review*, Vol. 60 No. 1, (January-February), pp. 105–114.

Officer, Lawrence H. and Samuel H. Williamson, 2014, "What Was the U.K. GDP Then?," MeasuringWorth, Available as spreadsheet download at: http://www.measuringworth.com/ukgdp/

Osborne, Michael J., 2010, "A Resolution to the NPV-IRR Debate?," *The Quarterly Review of Economics and Finance*, Vol. 50 No. 2, (May), pp. 234–239.

Osborne, Michael J., 2014, *Multiple Interest Rate Analysis*, Palgrave MacMillan: London, England.

Santayana, George, 1905, *Reason in Common Sense* or *The Life of Reason*, Charles Scribner's Sons: New York, NY.

Sharpe, William F., 1964, "Capital Asset Prices: A Theory of Market Equilibrium under Conditions of Risk," *The Journal of Finance*, Vol. 19 No. 3, (September), pp. 425–442.

Smith, Geoffrey, 2015, "Anglo American's Slash & Burn Plan Rocks Stock Market," Available at: http://fortune.com/2015/12/08/anglo-americans-slash-burn-plan-rocks-stock-market/ (dated December 8, 2015; downloaded December 2015).

Steiner, Bob, 2007, *Mastering Financial Calculations*, Prentice Hall: Harlow, England.

Townsend, Matthew, 2015, "Nike Authorizes $12 Billion in Share Buybacks, Stock Split," Available at: http://www.bloomberg.com/ (dated November 20, 2015; downloaded November 2015).

Trainor, William J. Jr., 2008, "Leveraged ETFs: A Risky Double That Doesn't Multiply by Two," *CFA Digest*, Vol. 21 No. 5, (May), pp. 44–55.

Treynor, Jack L., 1961a, "Implications for the Theory of Finance," Unpublished Memorandum (subsumed by Treynor and Black, 1976).

Treynor, Jack L., 1961b, "Toward a Theory of Market Value of Risky Assets," Unpublished Memorandum (subsumed by Treynor and Black, 1976).

Treynor, Jack L., and Fischer Black, 1976, "Corporate Investment Decisions," in *Modern Developments in Financial Management*, ed. Stewart C. Myers, pp. 310–327, New York: Praeger Publishers.

Updegrave, Walter, 2011, "Jack Bogle: This is the most difficult time to invest." Available at: http://money.cnn.com/2010/12/31/pf/investing/jack_bogle.moneymag/index.htm

Vanguard, 2017a, *Vanguard Total World Stock ETF Profile.* Available at: https://personal.vanguard.com/ (downloaded July 2017).

Vanguard, 2017b, *Vanguard Total International Bond ETF Profile*, Available at: https://personal.vanguard.com/ (downloaded July 2017)

Williams, John Burr, 1979, *The Theory of Investment Value*, Flint Hill, VA: Fraser Publishing Company. (Originally published in 1938 by Harvard University Press.)

Williamson, Samuel H., 2014, "What Was the U.S. GDP Then?," MeasuringWorth, Available as spreadsheet download at: http://www.measuringworth.com/usgdp/

Zillow, 2014, "In Most Major Markets, Negative Equity Has Fallen By Half Since Peak of Crisis," Available at: http://zillow.mediaroom.com/2014-12-17-In-Most-Major-Markets-Negative-Equity-Has-Fallen-By-Half-Since-Peak-of-Crisis (dated December 17, 2014; downloaded October 2015).

Abbreviations

- APR *Annual percentage rate*
- AUM *Assets under management*
- BLS *Bureau of Labor Statistics*
- CA *Current assets*
- CAPEX *Capital expenditure*
- CAPM *Capital asset pricing model*
- CD *Certificate of deposit*
- CF *Cash flow*
- CFO *Chief Financial Officer*
- CL *Current liabilities*
- CPI *Consumer price index*
- DCF *Discounted cash flow*
- DDM *Dividend discount model*
- EAR *Effective annual rate*
- EBIT *Earnings before interest or tax*
- EBITDA *Earnings before interest, tax, depreciation and amortization*
- EPA *Environmental Protection Agency*
- ETF *Exchange-traded fund*

ABBREVIATIONS

- FB *Future Balance*
- FCF *Free cash flow*
- FD *Financial distress (costs)*
- FV *Future value*
- FX *Foreign exchange (i.e., foreign currency)*
- GDP *Gross domestic product*
- HP *Hewlett-Packard*
- IMC *Investment Management Certificate*
- IRR *Internal rate of return*
- LHS *Left-hand side*
- MBA *Master of Business Administration*
- MIT *Massachusetts Institute of Technology*
- N.Z. *New Zealand*
- NPV *Net present value*
- NWC *Net working capital*
- NYSE *New York Stock Exchange*
- OCF *Operating cash flow*
- P/E *Price-to-earnings (ratio)*
- PhD *Doctor of philosophy*
- PV *Present value*
- RHS *Right-hand side*
- SWM *Shareholder wealth maximization*
- TVM *Time value of money*
- U.K. *United Kingdom*
- U.S. *United States*
- WACC *Weighted average cost of capital*
- YTM *Yield to maturity*

Index

Heard on The Street:
Quantitative Questions from
Wall Street Job Interviews
Timothy Falcon Crack

PhD (MIT), MCom, PGDipCom,
BSc (HONS 1ˢᵗ Class), IMC

A must read! Over 210 quant questions collected from actual job interviews in investment banking, investment management, and options trading. The interviewers use the same questions year-after-year, and here they are—with solutions! These questions come from all types of interviews (corp. finance, sales and trading, quant research, etc.). The questions come from all levels of interviews (undergrad, MS, MBA, PhD). The latest edition also includes 170 non-quant actual interview questions, and a revised section on interview technique.

www.InvestmentBankingJobInterviews.com
timcrack@alum.mit.edu

Pocket Heard on The Street
Timothy Falcon Crack

*PhD (MIT), MCom, PGDipCom,
BSc (HONS 1st Class), IMC*

These two pocket-sized editions fit in your pocket or purse, and are easy to read on the subway, bus, train, or plane! They are a careful selection of the best questions from the full-sized edition of *Heard on The Street*. The red-covered edition has 75 quant questions, with detailed solutions. The yellow-covered edition has 20 brain teasers, 30 thinking questions, and over 100 non-quantitative questions. The brain teasers, and more than half the thinking questions have detailed solutions. The quant questions in the red edition usually require math/stats, but the brain teasers and "thinking questions" in the yellow edition usually require little or no math; the thinking questions are in between.

---

www.InvestmentBankingJobInterviews.com
timcrack@alum.mit.edu

Basic Black-Scholes:
Option Pricing and Trading
Timothy Falcon Crack

*PhD (MIT), MCom, PGDipCom,
BSc (HONS 1st Class), IMC*

Extremely clear explanations of Black-Scholes option pricing theory, and applications of theory to trading. Based on award-winning teaching at Indiana University. The presentation does not go far beyond basic Black-Scholes because a novice need not go far beyond Black-Scholes to make money, all high-level option pricing theory extends Black-Scholes, and other books go far beyond Black-Scholes without the firm foundations given here. Includes Bloomberg screens, expanded analysis of Black-Scholes interpretations, and downloadable spreadsheets to forecast profits and transactions costs, and to explore option sensitivities (the Greeks).

www.BasicBlackScholes.com
timcrack@alum.mit.edu

Foundations for Scientific Investing:
Capital Markets Intuition and
Critical Thinking Skills
Timothy Falcon Crack

*PhD (MIT), MCom, PGDipCom,
BSc (HONS 1ˢᵗ Class), IMC*

A firm foundation for thinking about and
conducting investment. It helps to build
capital markets intuition and critical thinking skills. Every investor needs these skills
to conduct confident, deliberate, and skep-
tical investment. This book is the product
of 25 years of investment experience and 20
painstaking years of destructive testing in
university classrooms. The integration of finance, economics, accounting, pure mathematics, statistics, numerical techniques, and
spreadsheets (or programming) make this an
ideal capstone course at the advanced undergraduate or masters/MBA level.

---

www.FoundationsForScientificInvesting.com
timcrack@alum.mit.edu

Foundations for Scientific Investing:
Multiple-Choice, Short Answer, and
Long-Answer Test Questions
Timothy Falcon Crack

*PhD (MIT), MCom, PGDipCom,
BSc (HONS 1st Class), IMC*

This book accompanies *Foundations for Scientific Investing*. It provides 580 test questions (455 multiple-choice and 125 short-answer questions), plus the long-answer questions already appearing in *Foundations for Scientific Investing*). Suggested solutions to the multiple-choice and short-answer questions are given. The multiple choice questions may also be useful as a test bank for instructors in any advanced investments class.

---

www.FoundationsForScientificInvesting.com
timcrack@alum.mit.edu

PUBREF:20180312:16:52.349,280.OU

www.ingramcontent.com/pod-product-compliance
Lightning Source LLC
Chambersburg PA
CBHW060258100426
42742CB00011B/1791

* 9 7 8 0 9 9 4 1 3 8 6 5 1 *